Every Day with Jesus

MAY/JUN 2017

The Promised Holy Spirit

'I will pour out my Spirit on all people.'
Joel 2:28

Selwyn Hughes
Revised and updated by Mick Brooks

© CWR 2016. Dated text previously published as *Every Day with Jesus: The Promise* (May/June 2003) by CWR.
This edition revised and updated for 2017 by Mick Brooks.

CWR, Waverley Abbey House, Waverley Lane, Farnham, Surrey GU9 8EP, UK Tel: 01252 784700
Email: mail@cwr.org.uk Registered Charity No. 294387. Registered Limited Company No. 1990308.

Cover image: Getty/D. Sharon Pruit Pink Sherbert Photography
Quiet Time image: Devanath
Printed in England by Linney Print

MIX
Paper from responsible sources
FSC® C015900

CWR

Every Day with Jesus is available in large print from CWR. It is also available on **audio and DAISY** in the UK and Eire for the sole use of those with a visual impairment worse than N12, or who are registered blind. For details please contact **Torch Trust for the Blind**, Tel: 01858 438260. Torch House, Torch Way, Northampton Road, Market Harborough LE16 9HL.

A word of
introduction...

How long can you hold your breath for? In February 2016, according to the Guinness World Records, a Spanish free diver held his breath for 24 minutes and three seconds. Not something that you should try at home!

'You can't see air but you know that it's there, every time you blow up a paper bag' was an often heard song in our home when our children were growing up. Fresh clean air is amazing, bordering on the miraculous, and it's fair to say we take it for granted – yet all life is dependent upon it. Rarely do we stop to think about it unless it's absent, or if it begins to move. Moving air can be calming and refreshing, or even exhilarating. It can be no coincidence that the Holy Spirit is described as 'the wind' or 'breath of God'. A life-sustaining gift from God.

It was at that first Pentecost when the Holy Spirit burst onto the scene like a 'mighty rushing wind', breathing life, strength, energy and boldness upon an unsuspecting world. The same Holy Spirit who broke into the lives of the Early Church is also available to all who desire His indwelling presence and power today.

In this issue, Selwyn highlights the work of the Spirit in our lives. He firmly believed that the more we understand what is available through the Spirit, and appropriate it, the richer our lives will be. His prayer for you would have been – as is mine – that you will experience a fresh move of the Holy Spirit in your life.

Mick Brooks, Consulting Editor

'The promise of promises'

FOR READING & MEDITATION – LUKE 24:36–49

'I am going to send you what my Father has promised' (v49)

The Old Testament is full of great and precious promises, but there is one promise that stands out from among them all. Jesus referred to it, somewhat affectionately I think, in the passage before us today as 'the Father's promise'. You could describe it as 'the promise of promises'. This 'promise of promises' was first given by God to the prophet Joel: 'And afterwards, I will pour out my Spirit on all people. Your sons and daughters will prophesy, your old men will dream dreams, your young men will see visions' (Joel 2:28).

Although the Holy Spirit was clearly at work in the lives of God's people in the Old Testament, the prophets eagerly looked forward to a far greater and more extensive work of the Spirit, as this promise of the prophet Joel reveals. Notice the words 'pour out'. The picture conjured up by them is of a heavy tropical rainstorm – not of a drizzle or even a shower. This mighty spiritual downpour from heaven not only enabled those first disciples to be powerful witnesses to the risen Christ, it would also enrich the entire relationship between God and His people from then onwards.

FURTHER STUDY

Isa. 44:1–5;
Ezek. 36:22–28;
Gal. 3:13–14

1. What do the prophets expect when the Spirit is poured out?

2. How and why has Christ redeemed us?

However, let's be careful that we do not use Joel's prophecy as if it has only been partially fulfilled and is still awaiting final fulfilment. Since Pentecost, the Spirit has been here in abundance. We have all of the Spirit that the early disciples had in the days recorded in the Acts of the Apostles. The question that we must address, though, is this: does the Spirit have all there is of us? Over the coming weeks we will seek to answer that question as we look at various aspects of the Holy Spirit's work in our lives.

Loving Father, help me to face this question honestly and openly. You have given Yourself to me through Your Holy Spirit without reserve. Help me give myself in equal measure. In Jesus' name. Amen.

'Rabbits became ferrets'

FOR READING & MEDITATION – MATTHEW 16:21–28

*'Jesus turned and said to Peter, "Get behind me, Satan!
You are a stumbling-block to me"' (v23)*

We said yesterday that the fulfilment of the Father's promise – the coming of the Holy Spirit at Pentecost – changed the entire nature of the relationship between God and His people. This change is seen most clearly when we look at the lives of the disciples before and after Pentecost.

Before Pentecost these men were wavering in their allegiance and patchy in their achievements. One moment they could celebrate that evil spirits were subject to them (Luke 10:17), yet after they failed to heal a boy with a demon they had to ask Jesus, 'Why couldn't we drive it out?' (Matt. 17:19). They were ready to go to Jerusalem and die with Christ, it seemed, but on the way they couldn't help quarrelling over who would have the first places in His kingdom (Luke 22:24). Simon Peter could whip out a sword and cut off the ear of one of the party who had come to arrest Jesus (John 18:10), and then later cower before the accusations of a serving maid (Luke 22:54–57). The enabling the disciples had received in the three and a half years they were with Jesus seemed to operate intermittently and shakily.

Then something quite wonderful happened: the promised Holy Spirit was poured out upon them. A divine reinforcement took place. Instantly they appear to have become new men doing a new work. In the words of one preacher: 'Rabbits became ferrets at Pentecost.' A new power was conferred on them and took residence, releasing them from their timidity, their fears and self-centredness. The Holy Spirit turned the tide for those vacillating disciples. Here in the twenty-first century He can turn the tide for us too.

FURTHER STUDY

Num. 11:23–29;
Acts 4:1–12,
32–35; 6:1–7

1. How does Peter demonstrate 'divine reinforcement'?

2. How did the first Christians show concern for others?

Father God, how desperately we need a spiritual turn of the tide in our land, our churches and our homes. Begin the work in me, dear Lord. Touch me afresh by Your Holy Spirit this day. In Jesus' name. Amen.

The power to unlock doors

'On the evening of that first day of the week... the disciples were together, with the doors locked for fear' (v19)

We continue reflecting on the turning point in the lives of the early disciples – these ordinary men who became extraordinary and did extraordinary things in an extraordinary Spirit. Some would say it was the resurrection of Jesus that turned the tide for them. However, although the resurrection was a landmark event that strengthened these discouraged disciples (and, of course, a key event in the unfolding of the gospel), it did not allay their fears and timidity. After the resurrection, we read in our text, the disciples were huddled behind locked doors 'for fear of the Jews'. Imagine it: Jesus had subdued the greatest enemy of the human race – death – and yet the disciples, who were witnesses to the resurrection, were paralysed by fear. Even the appearance of the risen Christ, it seems, did not produce transformation. Although that fear was eventually dispelled by Jesus showing them He was alive by many 'convincing proofs' (Acts 1:3), something else was needed – the empowering of the Holy Spirit.

A woman once drew my attention to Luke 24:52–53, which says that after the resurrection and following Christ's ascension to heaven the disciples 'returned to Jerusalem with great joy. And they stayed continually at the temple, praising God.' Indeed, the disciples were now praising God and waiting for His promise but they were not yet equipped to challenge the status quo and witness to the death and resurrection of Jesus. They had praise on their lips but needed the power in their hearts. That boldness came after the Holy Spirit fell upon them at Pentecost. Only divine power brought them out from behind locked doors.

FURTHER STUDY

Acts 4:13–22; 7:51–60

1. How do Peter and John exhibit courage rather than fear?

2. How does Stephen confront the issues of life and death?

Father God, forgive us if we are retreating behind locked doors when, in the Holy Spirit, we have all the resources we need to face whatever life brings. Help us leave locked doors for the open road. In Jesus' name. Amen.

Power from 'on high'

*'If every one of [the things Jesus did] were written down...
the whole world would not have room for the books' (v25)*

Consider this: if the gospel had ended with the message of Jesus' coming to earth, His death, resurrection and ascension to heaven, it would not have been the gospel – at least, not the full gospel. It probably wouldn't have spread around the world. A living dynamic empowerment was needed for the disciples to grasp the full significance of the events recorded in the Gospels. When the Spirit came that is what happened; the life behind the events came upon them and turned the world upside down. No amount of good news can transform us; the facts need to be set on fire in our hearts by the divine Spirit.

FURTHER STUDY

Isa. 32:14–20;
Luke 3:15–18;
Acts 4:23–31

1. What baptism by Jesus does John promise?

2. How did God answer the believers' prayer?

Many times in my life I have tried to imagine what the Christian faith would have been like without the Holy Spirit. We would have had the four Gospels without the upper room. John's Gospel ends, as we see from our reading today, with a verse that says, if all the things Jesus did were written down, one by one, no building would be large enough to hold the books describing His deeds. Suppose we just had this thought at the end of John's Gospel about the number of books needed to record all Jesus did but no Acts of the Apostles, would that have energised your soul? Without the Spirit's illumination, how would we have reacted to those words? As we said earlier, the life behind the events of the Gospels had to move inside the disciples. And He did at Pentecost.

It is important to recognise, however, that the power the disciples needed for transformation came from 'on high' (Luke 24:49). It was not something they had to discover within themselves; it was a power that came directly from the throne of God. And His resources are endless.

Father, thank You for reminding me that the strength I need is not something I have to cultivate within myself but I receive from 'on high'. I open my heart to receive more of You today. In Jesus' name. Amen.

CWR Ministry Events

PLEASE PRAY FOR THE TEAM

DATE	EVENT	PLACE	PRESENTER(S)
10, 17, 24, 31 May	Living Out of God's Story	Waverley Abbey House	Philip Greenslade with Andy Peck
18 May	Improving Your Team Dynamic	WAH	Andy Peck
20 May	Christ Empowered Living	WAH	Mick and Lynette Brooks
22–26 May	May Country Break	Pilgrim Hall	Pilgrim Hall team
27 May	Waverley Abbey College Open Day	PH	Waverley Abbey College team
1–3 Jun	Partners' Break	PH	Mick Brooks and the CWR team
7 Jun	Hearing What God is Saying through the Old Testament	WAH	Andy Peck
7, 14, 21 Jun	Living Out of God's Story	WAH	Philip Greenslade with Andy Peck
15 Jun	Discovering Your Spiritual Gifts	WAH	Andy Peck
21 Jun	Hearing What God is Saying through the New Testament	WAH	Andy Peck
22 Jun	Inspiring Women Summer Day: Walking in Unshakable Confidence	WAH	Jen Baker and the Inspiring Women team
24 Jun	Waverley Abbey College Open Day	WAH	Waverley Abbey College team
26–30 Jun	Introduction to Biblical Care and Counselling	PH	John Munt and Rosalyn Derges

Please pray for our students and tutors on our ongoing BA Counselling programme at Waverley Abbey College (which takes place at Waverley Abbey House and Pilgrim Hall), as well as our Certificate in Christian Counselling and MA Counselling qualifications.

We would also appreciate prayer for our ongoing ministry in Singapore and Cambodia, as well as the many regional events that we are embarking on this year.

For further information and a full list of CWR's courses, seminars and events, call +44 (0)1252 784719 or visit **www.cwr.org.uk/courses**

You can also download our free Prayer Track, which includes daily prayers, from **www.cwr.org.uk/free-resources**

Holy Spiritless Christianity

FOR READING & MEDITATION – ACTS 19:1–12

'[Paul] asked them, "Did you receive the Holy Spirit when you believed?" They answered, "No"' (v2)

Yesterday we wondered what the gospel would have been like if the disciples had not been empowered by the Holy Spirit. The passage before us today gives us a little glimpse of that. When Paul came to Ephesus he sensed there was something missing in this keen gathering of disciples, so his first question was, 'Did you receive the Holy Spirit when you believed?' The reply they gave was, 'No, we have not even heard that there is a Holy Spirit.' The 12 apostles who received the Holy Spirit at Pentecost were busy turning the world upside down but the 12 disciples at Ephesus were barely holding their own. They lacked the divine indwelling.

A prominent figure at Ephesus was Apollos who, we learn from the previous chapter, was 'a learned man, with a thorough knowledge of the Scriptures' (18:24). Yet though he taught about the Scriptures, he seems to have known nothing of the Spirit.

Apollos epitomises a highly trained church leader who is well educated in the Scriptures but lacks understanding of the Holy Spirit. He had received, we are told, the baptism of John (18:25), but not the baptism of fire promised by Jesus. He knew the outer baptism but not the inner baptism. The result was refined ineffectuality. He was effective to a degree, but not to the degree that he could be effective. Thank God for every leader who sticks close to the Bible. But how much more ought we to thank God for every one who not only preaches the Bible but who preaches in the power of the Holy Spirit. Leaders would do well to remember the words of a wise man Donald Gee, who said: 'All Word and no Spirit, we dry up. All Spirit and no Word, we blow up. Word and Spirit, we grow up.'

FURTHER STUDY

2 Sam. 23:1–4;
John 5:33–40;
2 Thess. 2:13–17

1. What inspired David?

2. How does Paul link the Spirit and the Word?

Father, save us from knowing only an outer baptism and nothing of an inner baptism. And grant to all who teach Your Word, I pray, the mighty empowerment of Your Spirit. In Jesus' name. Amen.

Lighting up His face

FOR READING & MEDITATION – JOHN 16:12–16

'He will bring glory to me by taking from what is mine and making it known to you.' (v14)

Having reflected over the past few days on the importance of the Holy Spirit's coming to the world we now turn to consider the question: Just what was God's purpose in sending the Holy Spirit? Answering this question will take us to many aspects of the Spirit's ministry here on earth and will occupy our attention over the next few weeks.

The Spirit's very first ministry, as we see from our text today, is to glorify Christ. The great preacher C.H. Spurgeon wrote: 'It is the chief office of the Holy Spirit to glorify Christ... what the Holy Ghost does must be right for us to imitate... To what higher ends can we devote ourselves, than to something to which God the Holy Spirit devotes himself?' The goal of the Holy Spirit's coming is not to glorify the person who receives, nor the Person who is received, but to glorify Jesus.

One evening while I was in India, as I was being driven back to my hotel, we passed a procession. On a horse sat a man and a woman, and walking alongside were people who were shining torches on their faces. Intrigued by this, I asked the friend who was driving me what was happening. 'This couple have just got married,' he said, 'and friends and relations are shining their torches on their faces to draw everyone's attention to the fact that these two have now become man and wife. Tonight they are the centre of attention, they are the most important people in town.' How like the Holy Spirit, I thought to myself. The chief ministry of the Holy Spirit is to light up the face of Jesus. As the great apostle Paul reminds us, 'No-one can say, "Jesus is Lord," except by the Holy Spirit' (1 Cor. 12:3).

FURTHER STUDY

Isa. 63:11–14;
John 7:37–39;
Acts 2:29–36;
2 Cor. 3:16–18

1. How did the Holy Spirit glorify Jesus at Pentecost?

2. Whose glory do we reflect?

Heavenly Father, just as the Holy Spirit always seeks to glorify Christ, so may we do the same. Imbed this truth into our spirits that we are here for Christ's glory, not He for ours. In Jesus' name. Amen.

Our objective standard

FOR READING & MEDITATION – COLOSSIANS 1:15–23

'he is the beginning and the firstborn from among the dead, so that in everything he might have the supremacy.' (v18)

The truth that the Holy Spirit focuses our attention on Jesus saves us from going off at a tangent in our spiritual life. Imagine if the Spirit said: 'You no longer need to focus on Jesus. I am here to take His place. Forget about Him and concentrate on me.' This would present us with all kinds of difficulties, since it is very possible for the subconscious mind to give to the conscious mind suggestions which could easily be mistaken for the voice of the Spirit.

A man once informed me: 'The Spirit has told me to divorce my wife and marry another woman because this other woman has the gifts I need to multiply my ministry. I can be of far greater use to God with this woman than I can with my wife.' In response I told the man that he was quite wrong and that God would never call him to leave his wife for such a purpose. It was against the teaching of Jesus.

FURTHER STUDY

Acts 26:12–18;
Rev. 1:10–18

1. What clear vision of Jesus did Paul have?

2. What prostrated John at Jesus' feet?

When I was a pastor, there was a young woman in my church who belonged to a fiercely atheist family. Although she had given her life to Jesus, she claimed the Spirit had told her not to reveal to her family that she was now a Christian. Instead, she should just go along with their atheism and refrain from telling them she had become a follower of Jesus Christ. I explained to her that the voice she had heard was probably not the voice of the Spirit, for the message given did not fall in line with the teaching of Jesus. Christ said, 'whoever disowns me before men, I will disown him before my Father in heaven' (Matt. 10:33). Subconscious desires have to be tested and evaluated to check whether or not they agree with the teaching of Jesus – our objective standard.

Holy Spirit, so many voices can arise within me and easily be mistaken for Your voice. Give me a clear vision of Jesus so that I shall always decide according to Him. In His name I pray. Amen.

The test for all ministry

FOR READING & MEDITATION – JOHN 3:22–36

'He must become greater; I must become less.' (v30)

We are considering the truth that the first ministry of the Holy Spirit is to glorify Jesus. Keep this thought always in mind: that which does not glorify Jesus is not of the Holy Spirit, and that which is of the Holy Spirit invariably glorifies Jesus. If something appears to be very appealing to you but does not glorify Jesus then turn away. It is most likely something poisonous, and though it may charm you for a moment, it may wreak consequences for a lifetime. If it does not honour Jesus then run from it as fast as your feet will carry you.

Think carefully, too, whenever you feel you would like to support a so-called Christian cause. There are many ministries purporting to be Christian but they differ greatly from one another. A safe guide is this: the ministry that makes much of Jesus Christ is of the Holy Spirit, and the ministry which ignores Him, or keeps Him in the background, is not of the Spirit. If a particular form of teaching glorifies man, or even makes much of the Holy Spirit to the neglect of Jesus Christ, be wary of it. Jesus declared, 'He [the Holy Spirit] will bring glory to me' (John 16:14). C.H. Spurgeon once said of the Bible, 'I would rather speak five words out of this book than 50,000 words of the philosophers.'

All ministries must be subjected to this question: do they or do they not glorify Christ? If they do not they are not of the Holy Spirit. The poet Longfellow said that 'art is long' in his 'Psalm of Life', but longer still is the great art of lifting up Jesus. Are we willing to say, as did John the Baptist in our text for today, 'He must become greater; I must become less.'

FURTHER STUDY

Psa. 34:3;
2 Thess.
1:11–12;
1 Pet. 2:12–19

1. What did Paul pray for the Thessalonians, and why?

2. On whom does the Spirit of glory rest?

Father, grant that in everything I say and do for You I might learn the art of lifting up Jesus rather than myself. I long to live for Your glory, not my own. Help me to do that, my Father. In Jesus' name. Amen.

Revealed by the Spirit

FOR READING & MEDITATION – LUKE 1:46–55

'My soul glorifies the Lord and my spirit rejoices in God my Saviour'
(vv46–47)

How does the Holy Spirit glorify Christ? He knows that Christ's own accomplishments are what best glorifies Him, so He opens these things to our minds and hearts. Here, once again, is the statement Jesus made: 'He will bring glory to me by taking from what is mine and making it known to you' (John 16:14).

What did Jesus mean when He said the Spirit will take from 'what is mine'? He was referring, I believe, to His accomplishments on behalf of His people. There is a glory which He had with the Father before the world began (John 17:5), but in my opinion the glory He is thinking of here – the glory which He says 'is mine' – is the glory that comes from His birth at Bethlehem, His sinless life, His sacrificial death, His wonderful resurrection, His glorious ascension, His involvement in the outpouring of the Spirit and, of course, of His coming again. These are the things He can truly call 'mine'. The things that glorify Christ are in Christ. The Spirit draws on nothing from outside of Him but takes of the things of Christ and makes them known to us.

FURTHER STUDY

Psa. 36:7–8;
2 Cor. 4:3–7;
1 Pet. 2:4–12

1. What does the Spirit reveal to us?

2. Of what accomplishments does Peter speak?

When these things are made known to us by the Spirit, it is then that we can really begin to understand their true worth. Though many read about Jesus' coming to this world, their understanding is somehow clouded to the true significance of the events unless the Spirit reveals it to them. If the 'things' that belong to Christ are not revealed by the Spirit then they simply remain cold facts. When they are 'made known' by the Spirit then the truth comes alive. Those so favoured will say with the Virgin Mary, 'My soul glorifies the Lord and my spirit rejoices in God my Saviour.'

Dear Father, how can I ever thank You enough for revealing Jesus to me? Had Your Holy Spirit not done so my soul would still be in darkness. Now it is filled with light – Your light. I am eternally grateful. Amen.

It's all about Jesus

FOR READING & MEDITATION – 1 CORINTHIANS 2:1–16

*'The man without the Spirit does not accept the things...
from the Spirit... they are spiritually discerned.' (v14)*

One of the things that has amazed me as a preacher of the gospel is the way in which the Holy Spirit operates in people's hearts as the Word of Christ is shared and the Saviour's name lifted up.

Many years ago I used to get a little exasperated by a man who attended the church of which I was the pastor. After every service he would say: 'I don't see the point of all this preaching. You say the same things over and over again: Christ was born in Bethlehem, walked the earth, healed the sick, died on a cross, was resurrected and ascended to heaven, and is coming again. Aren't there other things that you can talk about, such as the state of the world and feeding the poor?' I knew my answers were not reaching him, but one night, as I was preaching on the cross, I saw the Holy Spirit gently lift the veil from his eyes and make known to him the wonders of Christ's undying love. He came forward to the front of the church at the end and said: 'Now I know what it's all about. It's all about Christ giving Himself for me... for me.' How was that accomplished? By my preaching? No. Oh, that played a small part, but the key element was the Spirit revealing the Word through human words. Through the written Word and by the spoken word, he saw the living Word.

FURTHER STUDY

Isa. 52:7–10;
Rom. 15:15–21;
1 Cor. 15:1–11;
1 Tim. 3:14–16

1. In what does Paul glory?

2. What is Paul's gospel?

Have you ever wondered how you were converted? It was through the Spirit taking the things of Christ and making them known to you. And He is still at work doing this. Perhaps at times you feel like jumping for joy as the Holy Spirit brings home to your heart a truth you thought you knew but suddenly you realise you have seen only half of it. The Spirit glorifies Jesus. Not you, not me, not even Himself. Jesus.

Heavenly Father, each day the truth becomes clearer: I would not know the real meaning of anything spiritual if the Holy Spirit had not revealed it to me. And all His revealing brings me closer to Jesus. For this I am deeply grateful. Amen.

Our Advocate within

FOR READING & MEDITATION – JOHN 14:15–21

'I will ask the Father, and he will give you another Counsellor to be with you... the Spirit of truth.' (vv16–17)

A significant phrase catches our attention as we move on to consider the Spirit's second ministry. That phrase is 'another Counsellor'. It is helpful to keep in mind that in the Greek language the word translated here as 'Counsellor' is *parakletos* or 'paraclete'. It is a combination of two words: *para*, meaning 'alongside', and *kaleo*, meaning 'to summon' or 'to call'. The thought in Jesus' mind when He told the disciples that the Father would give them another 'paraclete' is that after His death, resurrection and ascension to the Father, the Holy Spirit would come and be with them as their constant companion.

FURTHER STUDY

John 14:23–27; Rom. 8:26–30

1. What does Jesus promise to those who love Him?

2. How does the Holy Spirit help those who love God?

Parakletos is translated in the NIV as 'Counsellor'. Other translations use different words such as 'Comforter', 'Friend', 'Strengthener', 'Enabler', or 'Advocate'. My view is that the best translation is 'Advocate'. And I am not alone in thinking this. Many preachers and teachers also favour this word. An advocate is a legal representative who is required to do their best for their client and to plead their cause. However, in the Holy Spirit we have an advocate who operates on a higher level. An old hymn puts it well:

Christ is our Advocate on high,
Thou art our Advocate within.
O plead the truth, and make reply
To every argument of sin.

The Holy Spirit is an Advocate who does not merely do His best for us, He is the very best because He is the Spirit of truth and He pleads the cause of truth in our hearts against every argument that sin throws up.

Father, I am so grateful that You have provided for me not only an Advocate 'on high' but also an Advocate within. You are pressing Your Spirit on my spirit. For this I praise and thank You. Amen.

Looking for a counsellor?

When we meet people in life who are hurting, we can provide help and a listening ear. However, there are times when people need more than this. Perhaps they are struggling with a difficult issue and would benefit from professional counselling.

Wanting to help others is the very reason why Selwyn Hughes placed the importance of understanding God, ourselves and others at the heart of CWR's ministry. It is also why we have developed Higher Education counselling programmes and established Waverley Abbey College.

The college is now leading the way in Christian counselling training and to date has seen over 250 students graduate, many of whom have gone on to provide professional counselling services in both Christian and secular practice throughout the country.

Our Find a Counsellor directory serves to help people find a Waverley Abbey College trained counsellor in or near their local area. It is available on the website, along with more information about our counselling programmes and upcoming Open Days.

www.waverleyabbeycollege.ac.uk

WAVERLEY ABBEY
COLLEGE

'The arguments of sin'

FOR READING & MEDITATION – PSALM 51:1–19

'Do not cast me from your presence or take your Holy Spirit from me.' (v11)

We continue reflecting on the truth we touched on yesterday, namely that the Holy Spirit 'pleads the truth, and makes reply to every argument of sin'. 'The arguments of sin' – what did the hymn writer mean? Some psychologists might refer to this as the 'rationalisation of desire'. The following situation illustrates how this works.

You are angry and upset at someone who has injured you in some way or another. Your Christian conscience, guided by the Word of God, tells you that it is best to acknowledge the anger and put it away by handing the right to take vengeance over to God (see Rom. 12:19). But there is something within you that resists that idea – your carnal nature. So a conflict ensues. You are caught between your natural desire for revenge and your sanctified conscience, which tells you to take another way. It is at this point that the 'rationalisation of desire' begins. Since it feels good to harbour the thought of revenge you begin to think of reasons for your anger to justify the maintenance of that feeling. You tell yourself: 'I have a right to be angry. The person concerned needs to be taught a lesson so that he (or she) might not behave in the same way towards someone more vulnerable.' You might even persuade yourself that you can help God out by being His instrument for vengeance! But it is an evil desire – 'an argument of sin'.

Now, in the court of your soul at such a moment another voice is quietly speaking – pleading the truth and inviting you to take a different way, a more Christlike way. How much easier it would be for us to go our own way and to sin were it not for the ministry of the Paraclete in our hearts.

FURTHER STUDY

1 Cor. 10:1–13;
Gal. 6:7–11

1. What is the warning from Israel's history?
2. What is Paul's warning?

My Father, where would I be today if You had left me without a word in times of temptation? My life now might well have gone in the wrong direction. Your redemptions are my renewal. Thank You dear Father. Amen.

Imagination versus the will

FOR READING & MEDITATION – 2 SAMUEL 12:1–13

'Then Nathan said to David, "You are the man!"' (v7)

A biblical example of what we talked about yesterday – the 'rationalisation of desire' – is well illustrated by David and Bathsheba (see 2 Sam. 11). It is difficult to describe in detail in the space of this one short page all the profound wrongness of this, the greatest downfall of David's life. King David caught sight of the beautiful Bathsheba taking a bath on the rooftop of her home and was overcome with lust, desiring the woman for himself. Bathsheba was the wife of Uriah, one of his soldiers. While Uriah was away, David seduced Bathsheba and committed adultery with her.

How could a man who is described as a man after God's own heart (Acts 13:22) have done such a thing? Because of the rationalisation of desire – the arguments of sin. A wrong thought came into his mind (no one is exempt from that), but instead of blasting it with prayer he allowed his imagination to dwell upon it. Psychologists point out that the imagination is ten times more powerful than the will. The more David imagined what it would be like to sleep with Bathsheba, the more his will was weakened.

Then, fearing the consequences if his adultery was discovered, he 'arranged' the death of her husband and added murder to adultery. No doubt he told himself that Uriah had died in the discharge of his duty, and rationalisation led him to think of plausible reasons for his unworthy behaviour. So convinced was he by the arguments of sin, that God had to send the prophet Nathan to him with a barbed parable that broke through his defences. I dread to think what course David's life would have taken had God left him without a word.

FURTHER STUDY

Neh. 9:29–31;
1 Tim. 4:1–11;
James 1:13–18

1. How did the Holy Spirit warn Israel and how did Israel react?

2. What is Timothy commanded to teach?

Gracious Father, the more I ponder the Spirit's advocacy, the more my heart rises in adoration and praise for the provision You make for my continued salvation. Blessed be Your holy name forever. Amen.

Always there

'You, however, are controlled not by the sinful nature but by the Spirit, if the Spirit of God lives in you.' (v9)

For a few days we have been considering the advocacy of the Holy Spirit within. Have you ever been tempted to satisfy a desire at the expense of what is right and turned away? Why did you turn away? It was because the Holy Spirit was presenting truth to you and making reply to every argument of sin. If you are strong in virtue, if there are powerful defences within you that guard against the assaults of your own nature, if something keeps you back from the insidious influences of the world, it is because of the work of the Holy Spirit. Also bear in mind that He is constantly at work within you. He is always there.

FURTHER STUDY

Matt. 10:17–20;
Heb. 3:7–15

1. When would the Holy Spirit be at work within the disciples?

2. How does the Holy Spirit warn against unbelief?

In English law courts an advocate (usually referred to as a barrister) is required to wear a wig and a gown. The newspapers once reported an unusual incident during a trial at the Sheffield Quarter Sessions. Seeing that the advocate was not properly robed, the judge said, 'I cannot see you.' According to the law, a judge can see an advocate only when he or she is dressed in the correct manner. In this case the advocate appeared in court unprepared and was therefore chastised by the judge. What an unfortunate situation for the person on trial – no one to plead for them. Though it is Jesus who pleads for us before God the Father, rather than the Holy Spirit, I want to make clear that unlike the defendant in this illustration, you will never find no one is there for you, because the Holy Spirit is always there. Oh, you can silence Him, but He will be silent against His will. You can tell Him to go away, but He will go unwillingly. He knows the worst about you, but He is bent on saving you, no matter what the cost.

Lord God, help me stay alert to the whisperings of Your Spirit within my soul. When I am tempted, speak the word of life to my heart. I know You will never leave me. May I never leave You. In Jesus' name. Amen.

Building tomorrow's Church
today

Today, there is an urgent need in the lives of Christian young adults: a hunger for authentic biblical teaching. Yet there is also a disengagement with the Church and the more traditional methods of Bible reading.

In order to help build tomorrow's Church today, we want to do all we can to help young adults connect with God and the Bible in a way that is accessible, practical and relatable.

 24-7 PRAYER

We have the opportunity to address this by partnering with the charity 24-7 Prayer, who already work with young adults all around the world. By joining with them – bringing our 50 years' experience of helping people engage with God's Word – we are going to create and make available a new, generation-transforming resource.

We want to urgently begin work on developing and launching an app for mobile devices that will enable those between 18 and 30 to benefit from encountering Scripture daily in a unique way.

If you would like to prayerfully make a donation to help us equip this generation to live with God's Word at the centre of their lives and relationships, please fill in the 'Gift to CWR' section on the order form at the back of these notes, or visit **www.cwr.org.uk/donate**

'True truth'

FOR READING & MEDITATION – ACTS 28:1–10

'But Paul shook the snake off into the fire and suffered no ill effects.'
(v5)

We began this section by drawing attention to the text 'I will ask the Father, and he will give you another Counsellor to be with you for ever – the Spirit of truth' (John 14:16–17). Now we will look in more detail at that last phrase: 'the Spirit of truth'. The Holy Spirit never misleads – He is nothing but reality. He does more than bring truth; He is truth – the same truth that we find in Jesus. He will do nothing unless it is in conformity with the truth. And this truth is not truth as we might see it but as God sees it – what Francis Schaeffer used to call 'true truth'.

FURTHER STUDY

Isa. 45:18–25;
2 Pet. 1:19–21;
1 John 5:6–12

1. Who inspired prophets?
2. What is God's testimony about His Son by His Spirit?

Once when I was in America, I read about a group in one of the Southern states who allowed a young girl to be bitten by a snake in order that the power of God might be manifested in her healing. This group claimed that they had been prompted by the Holy Spirit to prove the 'truth' of these words in Mark's Gospel: 'they will pick up snakes with their hands… it will not hurt them at all' (Mark 16:18). Tragically, the child died. They took what is true – a statement of Scripture – but failed to apply it according to the truth. Sadly, they were being led not by the Holy Spirit but by their own spirits. In today's reading, Paul shook a viper into the fire and was unharmed, but he was bitten in the course of his ministry. Had he allowed a poisonous snake to bite him to prove Jesus' miraculous intervention and then survived, that would have given the Christian faith an unfortunate twist – the magical would have replaced the moral.

We need never worry that the Holy Spirit will ask us to do something that is not in accordance with the truth. Others bring truths; He is truth.

Father, to be under the influence of the Holy Spirit, who makes us more like Christ, is the greatest longing of my life. Surely this is the highest goal possible. May the Holy Spirit continue this work in me. Amen.

The Chief Witness

FOR READING & MEDITATION – JOHN 15:18–27

'When the Counsellor comes... the Spirit of truth who goes out from the Father, he will testify about me.' (v26)

The third aspect of the Spirit's ministry, as we see from today's passage, is to witness to Jesus and produce witnesses who do the same. To put it another way: the Holy Spirit is the Chief Witness to Jesus and is the creator of witnesses to Jesus. The promise given in today's text was fulfilled after the Holy Spirit came upon the disciples at Pentecost.

In Acts 5 we read that the apostles were put in prison for preaching the gospel. However, during the night an angel of the Lord opened the prison doors and told them to go and stand in the temple courts and 'tell the people the full message of this new life' (Acts 5:20). Later, when the apostles were brought before the authorities and asked why they had defied the instruction not to preach, Peter, the spokesman, said, 'We are witnesses of these things, and so is the Holy Spirit, whom God has given to those who obey him' (Acts 5:32). Notice the words 'we are witnesses... and so is the Holy Spirit'. The disciples and the Holy Spirit were working together for the same purpose – witnessing to the same Person with the same power.

FURTHER STUDY

Acts 8:30–40;
2 Cor. 6:1–10;
2 Pet. 1:16–18

1. In what way were the 'servants of God' witnesses?

2. Of what was Peter a witness?

Over the past few days we have explored the work of the Spirit as our Advocate pleading with us. But it is also true to say that the divine Paraclete pleads through us. He pleads through us to the men and women with whom we are in daily contact. Without His witness our witness can be futile. What is more, I think it is safe to say that the Holy Spirit not only unfolds truth but He unfolds persons also. By that I mean He makes us creative and effective. 'Wherever the Spirit is,' a Welsh preacher once said, 'creation continues.'

Lord God, live within me and give me a creative spirit. I surrender myself to You. Breathe new life into my life, so I might be creative and effective. In Jesus' name I ask it. Amen.

Convinced and convincing

FOR READING & MEDITATION – ACTS 14:1–7

'Paul and Barnabas spent considerable time there, speaking boldly for the Lord, who confirmed the message' (v3)

Yesterday we said that another reason why the Holy Spirit was given to the world was to witness to Jesus and enable others to do the same. Once I was asked to speak at a conference on evangelism on the topic 'What makes our witness to Jesus convincing?' In answer to that question I made several observations, but the chief one was this: what makes us convincing witnesses to Jesus is not the techniques we learn but the presence of the Holy Spirit in our heart and life.

Programmes and techniques can be helpful, but if the Holy Spirit is not working in us and through us as the Chief Witness to Jesus then all our words and efforts are often in vain. When we live our lives characterised by loving compassion, which seek justice promoting mercy and walking humbly with God, then the abiding Spirit within gives a strong sense of authority, and when we act, we act with the sum total of reality behind us. This sense of authority is lacking in many in today's Church because it can easily be explained as coming from our human spirit and is not convincing. What is needed is that inexplicable 'Plus' that only comes from the Holy Spirit.

FURTHER STUDY

Isa. 59:19–21;
Acts 10:34–46;
Rev. 19:5–10

1. What does God promise through Isaiah?

2. How convincing was Peter?

A Christian writer describes how he once saw a sign on a hotel that said 'Newly Furnished Rooms'. The letters were washed out and dim with age, and the hotel looked third rate and thoroughly dilapidated. There was no sign of newness. He picked up his pen and wrote: 'The sign was not convincing. It reminded me that there are many churches like that; they make you think not of good news, but of musty views.' Unless the convincing Spirit works through us, our words, however eloquent they may be, will convince no one.

Dear Holy Spirit, this is what I want – to speak for Jesus with the sense of authority that comes from You. I long not just to speak but to be spoken through. Grant that it may ever be so. Amen.

A face-lift

FOR READING & MEDITATION – ACTS 6:8–15

'All... looked intently at Stephen, and they saw that his face was like the face of an angel.' (v15)

In the light of what we said yesterday, perhaps each one of us ought to ask: Am I a convincing Christian? When I speak, is there a sense of authority in what I say? When I act, do I act with the sum total of reality behind me?

When I was a young Christian and working as an apprentice engineer, I listened as a Christian – a man much older and more experienced than I was – talked to someone about his need to give his life to Christ. His words made little impact because, as the man who was being witnessed to told me afterwards, 'His walk did not match his talk'. It was well known that the older Christian was 'light fingered' and stole things from the workshop and took them home. Others did too, of course, but his colleagues knew that a Christian should not act in that way. The voice of the Holy Spirit trying to plead through him was disrupted – disrupted and distorted because of his behaviour. The Spirit seeks not only to convince through our words but through our non-verbal communication also. By non-verbal communication I mean the things we convey through our actions. The indwelling of the Holy Spirit can make it apparent that we have been forgiven. Wasn't it Nietzsche, the famous philosopher, who said of Christians, 'for me to learn to have faith in their Redeemer... his disciples would have to look more redeemed!'?

The indwelling of the Holy Spirit gives us a face-lift, an inner assurance that makes us feel redeemed and reinforces every part of our personality so that we act in a way that reveals we are redeemed. It is the Spirit who makes the convinced convincing. May every one of us who names the name of Jesus be worthy of that name.

FURTHER STUDY

Acts 11:4–18;
Rom. 15:14–19;
2 Tim. 1:8–12

1. How did Peter convince the other apostles?

2. Of what was Paul convinced?

Father God, grant that Your Holy Spirit may so work in me that I will not only feel redeemed but also show that I have been redeemed. I am convinced, dear Lord. Now help me be convincing. For Jesus' sake. Amen.

'Whatever Became of Sin?'

FOR READING & MEDITATION – JOHN 16:5–11

'When he comes, he will convict the world of guilt in regard to sin and righteousness and judgment' (v8)

The Holy Spirit indwells us not only to make us convincing Christians but convicting Christians also. Our text for today tells us that one of the functions of the Holy Spirit is to convict the world of sin. How greatly this ministry is needed because, tragically, nowadays there is no acute sense of sin.

Some years ago, a secular psychiatrist wrote a book entitled *Whatever Became of Sin?* In it he made the case that in today's world people fail to realise that moral wrongdoing produces guilt and has a serious effect on the soul. A sin should be recognised as a sin, he says, and if the issue, with its accompanying guilt, is not dealt with in the right way – by recognising it as a sin, confessing it to whoever has been wronged and giving appropriate restitution – the unresolved guilt will sabotage all attempts made by therapists to deal with the problem.

FURTHER STUDY

Acts 8:14–24;
1 Cor. 5:1–5

1. For what sin did Peter rebuke Simon?

2. For what did Paul rebuke the Corinthians?

How strange and how sad that a secular psychiatrist should speak more plainly about sin than many church leaders. It is pointless to argue, as many do, that times have changed and that we are living in a different age. Such arguments are really efforts to deny or minimise guilt, and they are perilous because there is no way of dealing with the guilt that arises from crossing the boundaries of God's moral law other than by recognising that we have breached God's order and confessing to God the wrong that has been done.

The Holy Spirit wants to use us to convince the world of sin. You may argue: 'The challenge is too great. I am no advocate. How can I ever convince people who are so deeply ingrained in sin?' You can't. Not alone! You need the Holy Spirit to do it through you.

Father God, I have no skill at advocacy, but with all my heart I long for my life to firmly but graciously stand against sin wherever it is found – in my friends, my family and those with whom I work. In Jesus' name. Amen.

Egocentricity – the worst sin

FOR READING & MEDITATION – GALATIANS 2:11–21

*'I have been crucified with Christ and I no longer live,
but Christ lives in me.' (v20)*

Yesterday we said that what is needed today is an acute sense of sin. Terrible things happen and many people move on and think nothing of it. They are guilty of breaking their marriage vows, they take what does not belong to them, they lie and rage and blacken the character of others. You will come into contact with many today who treat such behaviour lightly; it only becomes wrong when it is discovered. Oh that the Holy Spirit would first free us from sin and then plead through us and convince others of sin and its lasting consequences.

Jesus assured the disciples that the Spirit would convict the world of three things: sin, righteousness, and judgment (John 16:8). He said, 'in regard to sin, because men do not believe in me' (John 16:9). This is a very important statement because it shows that the essence of sin is not believing in Christ – not making Him the centre of life. When we do not make Jesus the centre, then we make ourselves the centre – we take the place of God. Of all the sins that could be catalogued, surely none is worse than taking the place of God. Behaviours such as stealing, lying, cheating and adultery are certainly to be denounced, but the central sin is failing to let Jesus Christ be Lord of our lives.

Take away the first and last letters in the word 'sin' and what do you have left? 'I'. That perpendicular pronoun, as it has been called, points to the source of all our trouble. The greatest sin is putting the self in the place God has reserved for Himself. When that happens we disrupt God's design for our soul, which was made not to be egocentric but Christocentric.

FURTHER STUDY

Dan. 4:28–37;
Luke 12:13–21;
Acts 12:19–24

1. Trace Nebuchadnezzar's transition from being egocentric to God-centred.

2. What caused the deaths of both the rich man and Herod?

My Father and my God, I see that if I am to be a convincing living demonstration of Your life-giving Son, then sin must die in me and Christ must live in me. Grant that this shall be so. In Jesus' name. Amen.

Blocks or channels

FOR READING & MEDITATION – HEBREWS 12:14–29

'You have come to God, the judge of all men, to the spirits of righteous men made perfect' (v23)

We have seen how Jesus said the Holy Spirit would convict the world of sin, righteousness, and judgment. Having looked at the essence of sin – not believing in Christ – we move on to think about righteousness. Jesus' exact words are: 'in regard to righteousness, because I am going to the Father, where you can see me no longer' (John 16:10). Jesus is saying that His exaltation would prove that His righteousness – that is His complete obedience to His Father's will – had been accepted by His Father. And how the Holy Spirit longs to convince everyone that God will only accept us when we renounce our own righteousness and in repentance and faith accept the gift of Christ's righteousness.

FURTHER STUDY

John 3:18–21;
5:22–30;
Phil. 3:1–11;
Heb. 2:14–18

1. What has the Father entrusted to Jesus?

2. What did Paul consider loss for the sake of Christ?

Concerning judgment Jesus says, 'the prince of this world now stands condemned' (John 16:11). The ruler of this world – Satan – has been judged at the cross. Evil has met its match. We face no evil that has not been conquered by Christ on the cross. The Holy Spirit is at work in the world to convince men and women that they have no excuse when they say evil or the devil is too big a match for them. Satan is a defeated foe. The footprint of the Son of God is on his neck.

Though I have said this before it bears repeating: the first thing the Holy Spirit wants to do in us when we become Christians is to help us deal with any sin surviving in our souls, and then to plead through us, by our lives as well as our words, to those with whom we come in contact. Two people can speak the same words. The words of one will fall on deaf ears, the words of the other will fall on the heart. One is a channel of the Holy Spirit, the other a block.

Heavenly Father, with all my heart I ask that You will prevent me from becoming a block to Your Spirit. Make me a channel, I pray – someone through whom the Spirit can flow freely with no restrictions. In Jesus' name. Amen.

Praying in the Spirit

FOR READING & MEDITATION – EPHESIANS 6:10–20

'And pray in the Spirit on all occasions with all kinds of prayers and requests.' (v18)

The Spirit's fourth ministry, we discover from our reading, is to help us when we pray. Prayer, as you know, is at the heart of our faith. All communication with heaven begins in prayer. The more we pray, the more of God's resources we are able to receive into our souls. If you pray only a little, then only a little of His resources breaks through. A lot of prayer and a lot breaks through. Yet sadly, though our growth in Jesus depends so much on prayer, we are often disinclined to pray. Sometimes we have to force ourselves to our knees. The very thing we most need is that for which we frequently have little desire. How encouraging it is, then, to read in the passage before us today that we can pray in the Spirit.

FURTHER STUDY

Gen. 24:42–51;
Acts 10:1–8

1. How did guided prayer help Abraham's servant?

2. How did it help Cornelius?

But what does Paul mean when he tells us to pray in the Spirit? Some think we pray in the Spirit when we reach a certain level of prayer, for instance during times of particularly enthusiastic intercession. That, however, is not what the text is saying. We are told to pray in the Spirit on all occasions. Praying in the Spirit means to be prompted and guided by the Spirit, to pray with a definite dependence upon the Holy Spirit's leading.

There are different kinds of prayer – prayers of petition, of intercession and of thanksgiving – but all of our praying, regardless of its nature, is to be done in the power of the Spirit and by the direction of the Spirit. Terry Sisney, an American pastor, says: 'To pray in the Spirit one must be in the spirit of prayer, and that starts by accepting prayer as a God-given privilege and responsibility. No one will pray in the Spirit until prayer is important to them.'

Holy Spirit, I have come a long way in the school of prayer, but now I ask You to take me further still. Help me see prayer not just as important but as all-important. In Jesus' name. Amen.

When God says 'No'

FOR READING & MEDITATION – 2 CORINTHIANS 12:1–10

'Three times I pleaded with the Lord to take it away from me.' (v8)

It is vitally important that we see the need to be guided by the Holy Spirit when we pray. We need to continually ask Him to cleanse us from wrong ideas about prayer and to instruct us on how best to pray, for many of us are confused about this matter of prayer. Some think every prayer ought to be answered in the way we wish. Personally, I thank God for the prayer requests He has not granted because I have asked for things that would not have been a benefit to me spiritually. Are we willing to give all our prayers to the will of God and be as happy when God says 'No' as when He says 'Yes'. Our heavenly Father always gives the best to those who leave the choice to Him.

FURTHER STUDY

2 Sam. 7:1–11;
1 Chron.
22:6–8;
Acts 16:6–10

1. Over what did God say 'No' to David?

2. Over what did the Spirit say 'No' to Paul?

One preacher tells how a woman informed him she was leaving the church because her daughter had not passed an examination although, as she said, 'I have prayed harder for this than for any other thing in my life.' The girl not only failed the examination but unfortunately came bottom of the list! To the mother's mind that proved there was nothing in prayer and no point in coming to church any more. How different things would have been if the mother had followed the apostle Paul in today's reading and she hadn't insisted on her own way. How thankful we should be for Paul's words that sometimes God does refuse our requests because in His infinite wisdom His 'Nos' can help us grow in our trust in Him and in our experience of His grace.

Unless we allow the Holy Spirit to cleanse us from wrong ideas about prayer, our prayer life will result in irritation rather than illumination. It is right to ask God for things, but we must not be upset when He says 'No'.

My Father and my God, give me a trusting heart, and may I submit all my wants and desires to Your perfect will. Help me to take Your 'No' in the same spirit that I take Your 'Yes'. In Jesus' name. Amen.

A passion for prayer

FOR READING & MEDITATION – MATTHEW 7:1–12

'Ask and it will be given to you' (v7)

Yesterday we said that many people's thoughts concerning prayer are sometimes muddled. But perhaps you are saying to yourself right now, 'That's not my problem. I am quite clear about the importance of prayer and its purpose.' Then permit me to ask you this question: How much and how often do you pray? You see, it is possible to be clear about prayer yet inactive when it comes to the practice of it. How strange it is, as we said the other day, that though prayer is at the heart of our faith we procrastinate when it comes to actually praying. When did you last stay up late to pray? Maybe you say, 'I'm not very good at praying in the late hours of the day.' Well then: When did you last get up early to pray?

How do we overcome this weariness that affects so many of us when it comes to prayer? Bring the matter to God. Tell Him that you are convinced of the need for more prayer in your life but that often you have to force yourself to pray because the longing to pray is not as strong as it should be. Admitting and confessing your need often puts you in the way of having it met.

Many people do not receive things from God because they do not ask, even though in Scripture we are instructed to ask Him for things. But in addition to making such requests have you ever thought of asking Him to actually help you pray? I tell you what He will do. Through the Holy Spirit who dwells within you He will give you a spiritual passion and a deeper desire for prayer. Many Christians are floundering in prayer simply because they have never thought of asking for the Holy Spirit's help in praying. Do as you have been instructed: ask.

FURTHER STUDY

2 Chron. 30:12–20; James 1:2–8

1. Why did God hear Hezekiah's request?

2. Why does James encourage his readers to ask?

Lord God, light the flame of prayer on the altar of my heart in a new and fresh way. Take me deeper into You, dear Father, especially at the place of prayer. In Jesus' name I pray. Amen.

Prayer is powerful

In just a few months, churches and communities will gather to lift up their towns, villages and cities in prayer for the third annual National Prayer Weekend.

Last year, over 1,200 communities, from all over the world, handed out prayer request cards to their neighbours, schools, hospitals and businesses, asking them if they wanted prayer. The feedback we received from the National Prayer Weekend 2016 events has been amazing...

> *'All the received prayer requests were read out and prayed for. People walked in off the street asking for prayer. It has truly been an amazing time of seeing God at work in people's lives.'*

> *'We had a wonderful time of prayer when we covered the prayer requests that had been received. It was amazing how many requests came in!'*

If you plan to take part, or indeed are taking part in any other prayer event this year (such as Thy Kingdom Come, a prayer initiative launched by the Archbishops of Canterbury and York) here are some resources we have created especially for you. They make great giveaways and gifts as they explain more about prayer and introduce adults and children alike to the God who loves them.

Why Pray?

Rev Canon J.John guides readers through the Lord's Prayer, breaking it down into seven easy-to-follow phrases and using it explain more about why and how we can pray.

Living on a Prayer

Carla Harding and Pete Greig from 24-7 Prayer explore a contemporary and honest look at how effective prayer can be in our daily lives, introducing readers to prayer for perhaps the very first time.

Topz Tips for Prayer

The Topz Gang unpack the exciting topic of talking with God, helping children aged 7–11 discover the amazing gift of prayer with puzzles, stories and (of course) prayers!

Pens Special: Prayer

From saying sorry or thank you, to asking God for help or comfort – help young readers aged 3–6 understand more about the wonderful gift of prayer.

For more information on any of these great prayer resources, visit **www.cwr.org.uk/store**

A twofold secret

FOR READING & MEDITATION – PSALM 66:1–20

'Praise be to God, who has not rejected my prayer or withheld his love from me!' (v20)

Anyone who reads about the lives of godly men and women – for example, Martin Luther, John Wesley, John Henry Newman, Andrew Bonar, Amy Carmichael – is likely to be struck by the amount of time they spent in prayer each day. Frequently they would spend several hours at a time at the throne of grace, developing a close relationship with God and interceding for others. A careful reading of the biographies of the saints shows that their secret was twofold. First, they regarded prayer as vital, and second, they put a fence around certain hours of the day and reserved them for God.

FURTHER STUDY

Dan. 6:10–14;
Matt. 14:22–23;
Mark 1:35–39;
Luke 18:1

1. How was Daniel's day built around prayer?

2. What place did Jesus give to prayer?

Not only do we ask the Holy Spirit to help us pray but we also need to help ourselves. Christian growth is a combination of the Spirit's provocation and our pro-activeness. It's of vital importance to reflect on the importance of prayer until we are convinced that no part of our day is more important than the time we spend in prayer. Earlier I quoted Terry Sisney, the American pastor who said, 'No one will pray in the Spirit until prayer is important to them.' Think of what prayer achieves. It changes obstinate human nature. It challenges vice and fosters virtue. It brings heaven to earth. It succours souls in peril and brings comfort at the times of distress. It can be made for anyone, anywhere.

Once you become convinced of the prominence of prayer and commit to make it a priority, then you will not try to fit prayer into your day (as do most Christians) but will fit your day around prayer. You may have to rearrange your schedule but, believe me, your day will be quite different when it begins with prayer.

Father, in Your presence I am made into Your likeness. I long to emerge from my prayer times more alive to You, more alive to life, and more alive to others. Help me make prayer one of my first priorities. In Jesus' name. Amen.

Being prayed through

FOR READING & MEDITATION – ROMANS 8:18–27

'the Spirit himself intercedes for us with groans that words cannot express.' (v26)

Our text for today is one of the most astonishing verses in Scripture. It would appear from what Paul is saying in this verse that there are times when the Holy Spirit joins Himself to our spirit and prays in us and through us to God 'with groans that words cannot express'. Whether Paul means words that are unspoken or words of an unknown tongue we cannot be sure, but it would seem that there are times when an issue is so important that for a reason not known to us He prays in us and through us to the Father.

How strange this thought may seem to us. It sounds as if God is praying to Himself. A possible hint to what Paul is alluding to here is provided by this famous statement made by John Wesley: 'God does nothing redemptively in the world except through prayer.' Can it be that when God wants to bring about a change in the life of an individual, a family, a church, a community, or even a nation, and He is unable to get through to us, He will prompt His Spirit to do the praying in us, and through us, as the temple of His Spirit to bring to pass His purposes?

Many times in my life I have found myself burdened for something even though the details have not been clear. Perhaps you have had the same experience. The inexpressible yearning has astonished me; it is what some people call the infusion of prayer. You sense that you are not just praying but that you are being prayed through. The relationship between the Holy Spirit and God the Father is so close that the Holy Spirit's prayers need not be audible. The Spirit not only helps us pray but sometimes uses us as the vehicle through whom He prays – and His prayers may be with 'groans that words cannot express'.

FURTHER STUDY

1 Sam. 1:9–18;
1 Cor. 14:15

1. In what ways did Hannah pray?

2. In what ways did Paul pray?

Heavenly Father, that Your Holy Spirit can pray through me quite mystifies me, yet to doubt it is to question Your truthfulness. Help me understand this more deeply, dear Lord. In Jesus' name. Amen.

Blessed assurance!

FOR READING & MEDITATION – ROMANS 8:12–17

'The Spirit himself testifies with our spirit that we are God's children.'
(v16)

The Holy Spirit's fifth ministry is to assure the heart of every believer that he or she is saved and has been 'accepted in the beloved' (Eph.1:6, KJV). Can anything be more wonderful than to know beyond any shadow of doubt that we belong to God and are heirs of God and joint heirs with Jesus Christ? It is the Spirit who helps us know we are known and loved.

One of the questions that has been debated throughout the centuries by theologians and students is this: Can a man or woman have now, while they are here on earth, the assurance of personal salvation? This is not a question of mere speculative or academic interest raised in theological colleges; it is a question which goes right to the roots of spiritual experience. Indeed, this question is so profound that the answer to it determines whether or not a person is able to look upon himself or herself as a Christian in the New Testament sense at all. Yet many professing Christians seem divided on it. Please keep in mind that I am not talking about final salvation but having the assurance that one is saved now.

FURTHER STUDY

Gen. 15:1–6;
Gal. 3:26–4:7

1. What reassurance did God give Abraham?

2. What assurances does the Spirit give us?

A certain denomination claims this: 'It is not possible for a person to know with a certainty of faith that is not subject to illusion that he is a recipient of the grace of God.' Well, that is clear enough. But is it biblical? I absolutely believe not. The Bible contains a great many statements which make it clear that we can know now, in this present life, that we are the recipients of the grace of God and which give us the assurance that when we die we will go to heaven. When we commit ourselves to Jesus, He commits Himself to us. That is the good news. He gives us assurance – blessed assurance.

Dear Father, how thankful I am that Your Spirit witnesses with my spirit that I am a child of God. May this blessed assurance grow deeper each and every day. In Jesus' name. Amen.

Eternal life – now!

FOR READING & MEDITATION – JOHN 3:22–36

'Whoever believes in the Son has eternal life' (v36)

Yesterday we noted that one denomination says it is impossible to be certain about personal salvation. Others, although they do not go that far, believe that it is presumptuous and an indication of spiritual pride and religious complacency to say one is a recipient of the grace of God. One can say, 'I am being saved,' or, 'I am trying to be saved,' or, 'I am hoping to be saved.' But one should not say, 'I am saved.'

Many people of the world regard the question of whether or not one can have the assurance of personal salvation here and now as irrelevant and a sign of spiritual self-absorption. This is how one television interviewer dealt with an evangelical Christian during a debate I watched on this subject: 'Don't you realise that society is having to deal with countless economic and social problems, each of which presses for an immediate solution? Yet here you are, absorbed with the condition of your own soul.' Turning to the others who shared his view, the interviewer asked, 'Doesn't that strike you as being selfish?' They nodded their heads in agreement. It is interesting to note that one definition of a Christian is 'Someone who knows he or she is saved.'

FURTHER STUDY

Col. 2:9–15;
1 John 5:13–21

1. What does Paul say we have now in Christ?

2. Of what does John encourage us to be certain?

Assurance of salvation is impossible, says one group. It is presumption to claim it, says another. To seek it is a sign of spiritual self-absorption, say the people of the world. We certainly need God's wisdom and grace in dealing with these questions but, present assurance of personal salvation is possible – whatever others may say. If there were no verse in the Bible other than the one before us today that would be enough. 'Whoever believes in the Son has eternal life.' Has!

Heavenly Father, I am so grateful that I need not search any further for life. In You I have it. Thank You, Father, for the assurance given to me by Your Holy Spirit. Blessed be Your holy name forever. Amen.

Greater presumption

FOR READING & MEDITATION – JOHN 6:41–59

'I tell you the truth, he who believes has everlasting life.' (v47)

Over the past couple of days we have noted three different views of personal salvation. The first view is that assurance is impossible. The second is that to have assurance of salvation is presumptuous. The third view is that to even reflect on it is a sign of spiritual self-absorption. At this juncture I could summon a whole host of witnesses from the Early Church fathers to modern-day teachers and theologians who are certain it is possible to have spiritual assurance here and now. But let me select just one – John Wesley.

FURTHER STUDY

John 1:10–18;
2 Pet. 1:1–4

1. What have we received in Christ?

2. What assurances does Peter give?

In a famous entry in his *Journal*, he tells us that on 24 May 1738 he went very reluctantly to a room in Aldersgate Street, London, where Luther's *Preface to the Epistle to the Romans* was being read. With rapt attention he listened to the Reformer's description of the change wrought in the human heart through God's grace, and he felt, as he listened, his own heart being strangely warmed. He wrote in his Journal: 'I felt I did trust in Christ, Christ alone, for salvation; and an assurance was given me that He had taken away my sins, even mine, and saved me from the law of sin and death.' Notice the words 'an assurance was given me'.

Wesley, then, had the assurance of personal salvation. How about you? Are you sure you are saved? Everyone who has come to Jesus can know with certainty that they are saved. A Christian once made this comment to someone who told him it was presumptuous to say he was saved: 'I think it is greater presumption for anyone professing to believe in Jesus not to say that they are saved when the Master Himself declares, "Verily, verily, I say unto you, He that believeth on me hath everlasting life."'

Heavenly Father, thank You that You've put the matter beyond all doubt in Your Word, and Your Spirit gives me complete assurance. May I know and be conscious of Your presence in my life today. Amen.

'Lopsided Christians'

FOR READING & MEDITATION – GALATIANS 5:16–26

*'the fruit of the Spirit is love, joy, peace, patience, kindness,
goodness, faithfulness, gentleness and self-control.' (vv22–23)*

We examined the fruit of the Spirit in last September/ October's issue of *Every Day with Jesus* but it is important to re-visit this vital, sixth work of the Holy Spirit, where He seeks to reproduce in us the lineaments of Christ's character. Jesus was perfect in character, and from the moment the Holy Spirit enters us at conversion a transformational journey begins as we become more and more like Him.

The fruit of the Spirit in today's passage is characterised by nine qualities, and has been referred to by more than one author as 'the portrait of Christ'. One person has said, 'Just as when light goes through a prism it breaks down into all the colours of the rainbow so, if you could put the life of Christ through a prism, it would break down into these nine characteristics.'

A truly Spirit-filled Christian demonstrates in a balanced way the qualities of love, joy, peace, patience, kindness, goodness, faithfulness, gentleness and self-control. Please notice that I said in a balanced way. Most of us (myself included) might acknowledge that a few of these qualities are operational in our lives, but listen carefully to this next statement: it is when they all function together that they constitute Christlikeness. To have some without the others is to be a lopsided Christian. The Spirit may give different gifts to different people, but when it comes to the fruit of the Spirit, He is working in our lives to produce the same fruit in us all. 'The mere recital of these Christian graces,' says John Stott, 'should be enough to make the mouth water and the heart beat faster.' It certainly will in those whose hearts long to be more and more like Jesus.

FURTHER STUDY

Isa. 42:1–4;
2 Pet. 1:5–11

1. What graces does God's Servant display?

2. How does Peter say we gain a balanced life?

Heavenly Father, make me more like Jesus I pray. May I not be a lopsided Christian who is content with just a few graces. I long to have them all. Work in me to that end. In Jesus' name. Amen.

The 'firstness' of love

FOR READING & MEDITATION – 1 CORINTHIANS 13:1–13

'And now these three remain: faith, hope and love.
But the greatest of these is love.' (v13)

We pursue a little further yesterday's discussion, namely that if we are failing to mature in the fruit of the Spirit then we are lopsided Christians. The Spirit is not comfortable, for example, if we demonstrate love for others but lack self-control, or if we manifest patience but are lacking in goodness.

None of us, of course, cultivate these graces to maturity in our own strength. It is not a matter of human cultivation but of divine transformation, which comes about when we let the Holy Spirit have His way within our hearts. It's worth noticing that when Paul talks about the activities of the flesh in Galatians 5:19–21 he calls them 'acts', but when talking about the graces of the Spirit he calls them 'fruit' (Gal. 5:22). 'Acts' points to something manufactured; 'fruit' points to something that grows and develops without self-effort. Moffatt's translation, speaking of the fruit of the Spirit, calls it 'the harvest of the Spirit' (Gal. 5:22), looking ahead to the finished product, the outcome. Having the Spirit within, and allowing Him to have the right of way in our lives, results in a quality of being with nine characteristics. And the first, we are told, is love.

FURTHER STUDY

John 15:1–10;
Rom. 13:8–10;
2 Pet. 3:18

1. How do we grow and bear fruit, according to Jesus?

2. What is the debt Paul says we owe each other?

Love is emphasised again by Paul in the chapter before us today. If we have the Spirit within us then we have love, and if we do not have love then the Holy Spirit does not have us. And this love is not an occasional attitude towards those who love us, but is an abiding quality which reaches out to everyone – even those who some might consider unlovely. Love is the pre-eminent Christian grace, and when it is lacking then everything else is lacking.

Father, I see that without love I am nothing. Help me to increase in love, for if I do then I will truly grow. In Jesus' name. Amen.

The inspired order

FOR READING & MEDITATION – COLOSSIANS 3:1–17

'Let the peace of Christ rule in your hearts, since as members of one body you were called to peace.' (v15)

We think now about the other aspects of the fruit of the Spirit and consider each briefly. The second aspect of the fruit of the Spirit which every Christian can know is joy. It is no accident that joy follows love, for joy is a by-product of love. If you seek joy first, it will elude you, but when you love then joy will follow. Joy is quite different from happiness. Happiness depends on whether or not whatever is happening happens happily. However, the Holy Spirit's presence can enable us to know joy even in the most unhappy circumstances.

The third aspect of the fruit of the Spirit is peace. The order is an inspired one: first love, then joy, then peace. 'Peace,' it has been said, 'is joy grown quiet and assured.' The peace which is of the fruit of the Spirit not only endures regardless of what happens but it calmly waits to see how God will turn each situation to good. This is the peace Jesus had. He faced everything that life threw at Him and turned it to good. This peace is a peace that never goes to pieces.

The fourth quality of the Spirit's fruit is patience. Moffatt translates this as 'good temper'. The King James Version uses the word 'longsuffering'. Patience is love stretched out. It is so elastic and so tough that it doesn't break down into bad temper. It maintains good temper in the middle of all of life's ups and downs. A friend of mine says: 'You can always tell whether a person is patient or impatient by the way he or she honks the horn of their car. The Christian way calls attention to a situation; the unchristian way not only calls attention to a situation but it also calls attention to what the honker feels about the situation.'

FURTHER STUDY

Psa. 16:1–11;
Rom. 14:15–21;
James 3:13–18

1. What produces joy and leads to peace?

2. What flows from heavenly wisdom?

Lord God, give me a heart that is unperturbed amid provocation and remains sweet amid surrounding bitterness. Help me be the one who is peaceful in times of stress; at rest amid restlessness. In Jesus' name. Amen.

The flavour of Pentecost

FOR READING & MEDITATION – EPHESIANS 5:1–17

'Live as children of light (for the fruit of the light consists in all goodness, righteousness and truth)' (vv8–9)

How appropriate on Pentecost Sunday to arrive at the middle quality of the fruit of the Spirit – kindness – which some commentators believe is central because it puts flavour in all the others. The interesting thing about kindness is that we remember an act of kindness when all other events have been forgotten. Luke, writing about Paul's shipwreck on Malta, felt it was important to include a notable kind act: 'The natives,' he said, 'showed us uncommon kindness' (Acts 28:2, Moffatt). God lets His kindly rain fall on the evil and the good (Matt. 5:45). The person who is filled with the Spirit will also rain kindness on all, regardless.

FURTHER STUDY

2 Sam. 9:1–11;
Prov. 3:1–6;
Acts 11:22–26

1. How did David show God's kindness?

2. How did Barnabas demonstrate the fruit of the Spirit?

The sixth quality of the Spirit's fruit is goodness. This is perhaps the hardest to define. Sometimes it is translated 'generosity'. We are all aware of the term 'do-gooder', which is used of those who do good for the pleasant feelings they get. The goodness which is an aspect of the fruit of the Spirit, however, causes us to do good to people, not so we will be noticed but so that God will be praised (Matt. 5:16). It was said of Jesus that 'he went around doing good and healing all who were under the power of the devil' (Acts 10:38). But He did not do it for the pay-off – good feelings – but because He wanted to do the will of the Father. And that's what the Spirit wants to happen with us.

The seventh aspect of the fruit of the Spirit is faithfulness. This word is best translated 'fidelity' and refers to someone who is trustworthy, reliable and utterly dependable – a faithful steward of time, talents and possessions. In heaven there is a special 'thank you' awaiting those who are faithful (see Matt. 25:21).

Father, how I long to display Your kindness and goodness and be someone who is faithful in each area of my life. May this fruit of the Holy Spirit grow in me day by day. In Jesus' name. Amen.

Happiness second

FOR READING & MEDITATION – ROMANS 6:1–14

'We were... buried with him through baptism into death in order that... we too may live a new life.' (v4)

We consider now the last two qualities of the fruit of the Spirit – gentleness and self-control. The Greek word translated 'gentleness' has no exact equivalent in English. As well as being translated 'gentleness' it can also be translated 'meekness' or even 'humility'. The person in whom the Spirit dwells will be gentle, meek and humble. We need to think about all three words if we are to understand this quality. Gentleness suggests avoiding any heavy-handedness in our dealings with others. Meekness indicates the absence of pride, and humility the absence of any sense of superiority.

Last in Paul's list of the fruit of the Spirit is self-control. The word implies a fine mastery of self and is used to describe someone who is controlled, disciplined and obedient to the will of God. Isn't it interesting that the list of the fruit of the Spirit begins with love and ends with self-control? The two are complementary. How can we give ourselves in love unless we have self-control? It's as we learn to serve and give ourselves to God first that we can then offer ourselves in service to others.

All nine aspects of the fruit of the Spirit, as we have said, were evident in the life of Jesus; in Him they ripened to perfection. One commentator says, 'This list of fruits of the Spirit provides us with one of the greatest visions of holiness in the New Testament.' It's important to remember that God's purpose for our lives is not first to make us happy, but holy. And when we aim for holiness first, then happiness will follow as a consequence. We shouldn't be surprised that holiness is the result when the Spirit dwells in us; He is, after all, the Holy Spirit.

FURTHER STUDY

Matt. 11:25–30;
2 Cor. 10:1;
2 Tim. 1:3–7

1. How can we learn from Jesus?

2. What characterises the Spirit that God gives?

Blessed Holy Spirit, help me take every opportunity to demonstrate the fruit of the Spirit which, by Your grace and power, You are developing within me. In Jesus' name. Amen.

Power: walk carefully

'But everything should be done in a fitting and orderly way.' (v40)

The seventh work of the Spirit is to bestow Christ's Church with supernatural gifts. Here we enter an arena that is strewn with the scalps of many a theological gladiator, and there is deep division in parts of the Church on the gifts of the Spirit. Although many sincere Bible-believing Christians hold the view that some supernatural gifts such as recorded here in 1 Corinthians 12 and 14 were given only for the founding of the Church, my own view is that this cannot be supported by Scripture and my following commentary reflects this view.

FURTHER STUDY

Acts 2:1–6;
2:17–21;
Gal. 3:1–5

1. What gifts came with the gift of the Spirit?

2. How is the Holy Spirit received?

Then there are those who accept that there are spiritual gifts but downplay them in favour of the fruit of the Spirit. They emphasise purity but at the expense of power – an equally important emphasis. Others in the Church regard the gifts of the Spirit as an extension of our natural abilities and thus deny their supernatural nature. For example, Christians who hold this view would see the 'message of wisdom' (12:8) as being not supernatural wisdom but natural wisdom gained from life experience and used by the Holy Spirit for a divine purpose.

Let me be quite clear what I believe the nature of the gifts are in 1 Corinthians 12: the gifts of the Spirit here are not an extension of our natural powers but are given to us by the Spirit. They do not rise up from within but come down to us from above. Many Christians avoid the gifts of the Spirit because of the possibility that disorderliness will follow – which was a problem in the Corinthian church. But when some coals fall out of the grate the answer is not to get a fire extinguisher and put out the fire but rather to reach for a pair of tongs and put the coals back.

Dear Father, help us as Your people to be open to all Your Holy Spirit wants to give us, and to have the courage not to withdraw in the face of excess but to deal with matters that arise firmly yet lovingly. In Jesus' name. Amen.

Congratulations! You're gifted

FOR READING & MEDITATION – ROMANS 12:1–8

*'I urge you, brothers, in view of God's mercy, to offer your bodies
as living sacrifices' (v1)*

In order to understand the place the gifts of the Spirit have, it is necessary to compare them with other gifts mentioned in the New Testament. The Bible teaches, as I understand it, that three main streams of gifts are given to the Church. The first stream is outlined in the section before us today. The seven gifts in Romans are, in my opinion, natural talents built into our personalities by a gracious God as part of His gift of creation. These I call basic gifts.* Our natural abilities are anointed by the Spirit at conversion and are then used for spiritual purposes. Let's explore them one by one.

(1) Prophesying: this has to do with persuasiveness in the presentation of the truth. (2) Serving: this is a God-given ability to be aware and understand the personal needs of others and minister to them in the most helpful ways. (3) Teaching: this is the ability to present truth clearly and accurately. (4) Encouraging: this is the ability to come alongside those who are hurting and stimulate their faith with encouraging words or actions.

(5) Contributing: this is the ability to organise our personal lives in such a way that we are able to give financially to others' needs. (6) Leadership: this is the ability to co-ordinate the activities of others for the achievement of a common goal. (7) Showing mercy: this is the ability to empathise deeply with the misfortunes of others and give them mental and emotional support.

Everyone, I believe, has at least one of these seven gifts. And every one of us has a responsibility to find out what our gift is.

FURTHER STUDY

Exod. 31:1–11;
Dan. 1:17–21;
1 Pet. 4:7–11

1. What natural gifts did the Spirit utilise in building the tabernacle?

2. How does Peter say we administer the grace of God?

Father, help me be clear as to which gift You have built into me by creation. I dedicate myself afresh to that task today. Please reveal my gift to me. In Jesus' name. Amen.

*To help you discover what your basic gift is and for more on this subject, click on 'Discovering your basic gift' at www.cwr.org.uk/free-resources

The supernatural gifts

'Now to each one the manifestation of the Spirit is given for the common good.' (v7)

Yesterday we said that there are three streams of gifts found in the New Testament. These are the gifts of God, the gifts of the Spirit, and the gifts which Jesus gives to His Church. Having examined the gifts of God given through creation, we now examine those gifts which are commonly called the 'gifts of the Spirit'.

(1) Wisdom: a supernatural revelation given to someone for the purpose of resolving an issue that baffles human wisdom. (2) Knowledge: this is not human knowledge but a supernatural insight given by the Spirit for a spiritual purpose. (3) Faith: the supernatural ability to 'believe' for something beyond one's own natural faith. (4) Gifts of healing: a supernatural empowerment given to a believer to bring healing for those unwell. (5) Miraculous powers: the supernatural ability to perform miracles. (6) Prophecy: the ability to supernaturally convey a message from God that addresses a particular issue at a particular time (eg Agabus in Acts 11:27–30). (7) Distinguishing between spirits: the supernatural ability to discern the source of a spiritual manifestation, whether it be the human spirit, the Holy Spirit or a demonic spirit. (8) Speaking in different kinds of tongues: the supernatural ability to speak in a language never learned. (9) Interpretation of tongues: the supernatural ability to interpret a message given in tongues.

FURTHER STUDY

1 Kings 3:7–12, 28;
Zech. 4:1–6;
Acts 10:9–20;
1 Thess. 1:5;
Heb. 2:1–4

1. How was Peter directed by the Holy Spirit?

2. How is the Trinity active in the preaching of the gospel?

I have emphasised the word 'supernatural' quite deliberately for, although every work of God is supernatural, especially His work of conversion, there are times when He wants to use these supernatural gifts of the Spirit to fulfil His purposes.

Gracious and loving Father, forgive us that we are prone to rely on our own resources rather than on Your resources. Forgive us, too, for our fear of the supernatural. In Jesus' name. Amen.

The ministry gifts

FOR READING & MEDITATION – EPHESIANS 4:1–16

'When he ascended on high, he led captives in his train and gave gifts to men.' (v8)

We consider now the third stream of gifts – the gifts which the ascended Christ gives to His Church. The gifts of God in Romans 12 are 'natural' talents that the Holy Spirit anoints. The gifts in 1 Corinthians 12 are specific gifts that the Holy Spirit distributes as He determines. This third stream which we will explore now – gifts given by Christ – are to fulfil specific roles in His Church. Let's consider them one by one.

(1) Apostle: this person has the gift of pioneering new territory for the gospel. (2) Prophet: this person will be gifted to elevate the spiritual vision of the Church. (3) Evangelist: a person with the gift of being able to reach people with the message of salvation in Christ. (4) Pastor and teacher: the gift of being able to shepherd the flock of God and explain the truths of God's Word clearly in order to bring people to maturity and to equip them for service.

FURTHER STUDY

Acts 11:27–30; 13:1–2; 1 Pet. 5:1–11

1. Why are prophets needed in the Church?

2. What should characterise leaders, according to Peter?

There are similarities between all three streams of gifts; they are all intended, for example, for the building up of the body of Christ – the Church – and they are all gifts of divine grace. There are dissimilarities also. For example, in my opinion although the Greek word translated 'prophecy' is the same in Romans 12, 1 Corinthians 12 and Ephesians 4, there is a difference in the demonstration and exercise of this gift. Prophecy in Romans 12 is the natural gift of speaking persuasively, anointed by the Spirit. Prophecy in 1 Corinthians 12 is the supernatural gift of receiving words directly from the Spirit for specific situations. In Ephesians 4 the gift is wrapped up in a person. The person is the gift.

Lord Jesus, thank You for the way You have selected certain people for the task of building up Your Church and for putting them in the right place. Anoint them with Your heavenly wisdom. For Your own dear name's sake. Amen.

'Not in my back yard'

FOR READING & MEDITATION – 1 CORINTHIANS 16:1–14

'Do everything in love.' (v14)

FURTHER STUDY

1 Cor. 1:4–9;
1 Thess.
5:12–24;
Heb. 13:20–21

1. How does Paul view the Corinthians' possession of spiritual gifts?

2. How were the Thessalonians exhorted to use spiritual gifts?

Having looked in the past few days at the three streams of gifts in the New Testament, we focus again on the gifts of the Spirit in 1 Corinthians 12. Earlier we recognised that Christians hold differing views on the gifts of the Spirit, but by far the greatest difficulty, I have found, is that the gifts are supernatural.

Whenever we touch upon the supernatural we quickly find ourselves out of our depth, and there is something about human nature that likes very much to be in control. Many quite willingly accept the fact of the supernatural, but only in theory. It's fine, they say, as long as it is not expressed in their back yard. A minister once confessed: 'I believe the gifts of the Spirit are meant to be an everyday part of church life, but I'm scared stiff of them ever making an appearance in my church. I just wouldn't know how to handle them.' Fear, I believe, plays a great part in many people's reluctance to teach and encourage believers to open themselves to the gifts of the Spirit.

The remedy for this is to teach believers the importance of love. There is a good reason why 1 Corinthians 13 is sandwiched between 1 Corinthians 12 and 14. It is possible, says Paul, to have a variety of gifts, but if we do not demonstrate these with love then we are nothing more than 'a resounding gong or a clanging cymbal' (v1). If a church emphasises the need for love to underlay all expressions of gifts it need not fear opening up to the Spirit. When love wanes then disorder reigns. Paul's words sum up the matter for us: 'Follow the way of love and eagerly desire spiritual gifts' (1 Cor. 14:1).

Gracious God, help us not to fear Your supernatural work. May we draw from Your Holy Spirit all He desires to give us, but guide us also so that we experience all You have to give us without going to excess. In Jesus' name. Amen.

Everything!

FOR READING & MEDITATION – JOHN 14:25–31

'the Holy Spirit... will teach you all things and will remind you of everything I have said to you.' (v26)

The eighth work of the Holy Spirit is to be our teacher and, to use an unusual word, our 'remembrancer'. Today's verse tells us that the Holy Spirit taught and brought to the memory of the apostles Jesus' words so they could record them for us in the New Testament. Over the next few days we will consider how the Holy Spirit teaches us and reminds us of the words that He originally inspired in the Bible.

One commentator says of today's text: 'Here is both conservatism and radicalism. The Spirit conserves all that Jesus has taught and opens us up to the universalism of Jesus by applying to the whole of life the things He taught.' Christianity shows us the real meaning of radical – it turns men and women inside out and puts them the right way up. Nothing in life is as revolutionary as the Christian message.

Notice again Jesus' words: 'The Holy Spirit will teach you all things and will remind you of everything I have said to you.' 'Everything I have said to you.' Everything! When we stray from the Holy Spirit's guidance we have a tendency to fasten on to one or two aspects of what Jesus taught and ignore the 'everything'. The consequence is an unbalanced form of Christianity with an overemphasis on some things and an underemphasis on others. Some churches known to me are built on one truth which they constantly teach to the neglect of other truths that are equally important. They live on one truth instead of the whole truth. This is why in some churches there are Christians who are controversial; they have to be controversial to justify their imbalance. Christians who are under the control of the Spirit are not controversial but creative.

FURTHER STUDY

Acts 20:17–35

1. What importance did Paul attach to the 'whole' truth?

2. What words of Jesus did he recall?

Spirit of God, take from my heart the tendency to live by one truth or even a small number of truths. I want my life to be based on the whole truth as it is in Christ Jesus. For His dear name's sake I pray. Amen.

Fixed – yet unfolding

FOR READING & MEDITATION – EPHESIANS 4:1–16

'As a prisoner for the Lord, then, I urge you to live a life worthy of the calling you have received.' (v1)

Jesus' promise that when the Holy Spirit came He would be our teacher is incredibly important. But just how would He be our teacher? Is Jesus saying that the Holy Spirit would reveal new things to us or that He would make clear to us the teaching which He had already given? There is a sense in which it must be both if we remember that He will never reveal anything to us which is not in accord with His Word.

A prominent agnostic once claimed that Christianity and science could never be reconciled because science is never fixed, whereas Christianity is fixed in its absolutes and dogmas. His claim is only true in part. Christianity is fixed – yet it is unfolding. Concerning the coming of the Holy Spirit, Jesus made it clear that He would always act and speak in ways that were in harmony with His own spirit. That part of His ministry was fixed. But through men like the apostle Paul, He unpacked Jesus' teaching. For example, in today's passage he expanded, under the Holy Spirit's direction, Jesus' teaching about the structure of the Church and different roles within it. Since the New Testament was completed there has been no fresh revelation. However, the Holy Spirit continues to illuminate and unfold the words He has inspired.

FURTHER STUDY

Eph. 1:15–23;
Col. 1:28–2:8

1. Why do we need the Spirit of wisdom and revelation?

2. How necessary is it to continue as we began as believers?

When Jesus said, He 'will teach you all things,' He did not mean, as some have taken it, that the Holy Spirit would provide us with an encyclopaedic knowledge of all matters relating to heaven, earth and hell. The 'all things' relates to all that we need to know in order to live an effective life for Jesus here on the earth – all things pertaining to godliness.

Father, how glad I am that the Christian message is fixed and yet unfolding. This meets my deepest need, for I long to be established and yet spurred on to greater things. Blessed be Your name forever. Amen.

A teacher par excellence

FOR READING & MEDITATION – PSALM 25:1–7

'guide me in your truth and teach me, for you are God my Saviour'
(v5)

We continue reflecting on the words 'the Holy Spirit... will teach you all things' (John 14:26). John Stott suggests that 'in one sense we may say the teaching ministry of Jesus had proved a failure'. That sounds rather negative, but listen to his argument: 'Several times he had urged his disciples to humble themselves like a little child, but Simon Peter remained proud and self-confident. Often he had told them to love one another, but even John seems to have deserved his nickname "son of thunder" to the end.' John appears to have been one of the most loving of the disciples, but he wanted on one occasion to call fire down from heaven on the Samaritans who were resistant to our Lord spending the night amongst them. 'Lord, do you want us to call fire down from heaven to destroy them?' (Luke 9:54). Then we read: 'Jesus turned and rebuked them' (Luke 9:55). He rebuked them because of their unspiritual attitude.

Take Simon Peter. He was brash, impulsive, blustering, at times loud-mouthed. Yet when you read Peter's first letter you cannot help but notice how the man has been changed. He writes so much about submission and obedience and holiness that we wonder if this is the same Peter we read about in the Gospels.

And John, it seems, carried the nickname 'Son of Thunder' (Mark 3:17) right up to the time when Christ left them, but his letters are full of divine love. What brought about the difference in Peter and John? It can only have been the work of the Holy Spirit in their lives, who gave them a deeper understanding of what Jesus had taught. Clearly the Holy Spirit is a teacher par excellence.

FURTHER STUDY

1 Cor. 6:9–11;
Col. 1:9–14

1. What changes had some Corinthians undergone by the Spirit?

2. What does Paul pray the Spirit will do for us?

Father, through Your Holy Spirit You have taught me so much and brought about so much change in my life. For that I am deeply grateful. But is there need for more change? With all my heart I say 'Yes'. Teach me still more, dear Lord. Amen.

The words of Christ

FOR READING & MEDITATION – 1 TIMOTHY 6:1–10

'If anyone... does not agree to the sound instruction of our Lord Jesus Christ... he is conceited' (vv3–4)

Jesus said the Holy Spirit would not only be our teacher but, as we saw, our 'remembrancer' also: 'the Holy Spirit... will remind you of everything I have said to you' (John 14:26). I don't know about you, but I find the idea of the Spirit reminding us about everything Jesus said to be tremendously comforting and encouraging.

For this to happen, of course, we first need to be familiar with everything that has been recorded of what Jesus said, for the Spirit cannot bring His sayings to our remembrance if we don't know them. This is why it is important in our reading of Scripture to focus on the words of Christ. Many Bibles print Jesus' words in red, which I find very helpful. Whenever I read the Gospels and see the words of Jesus in red something clicks inside of me and says, 'Read these words carefully, for they are the actual words of our Saviour, which He spoke when He was here on earth.' You may be interested to know that J.B. Phillips translates the words of today's text in this way: 'If anyone tries to teach some doctrinal novelty which is not compatible with sound teaching (which we base on Christ's own words and which leads to Christ-like living), then he is a conceited idiot!' Notice the phrase 'Christ's own words'.

FURTHER STUDY

John 6:60–69;
1 Cor. 11:23–26;
Rev. 22:6–9,
18–21

1. Why are the words of Jesus important?

2. Reflect on the words of Jesus that Paul received.

Dr Larry Crabb says: 'When dreams shatter, when terrorists win and marriages fail, the Spirit is not silent. He reminds us that what matters most is unthreatened. The Father's agenda is on track.' If we are prepared to spend time reading and meditating on Scripture – particularly the things Jesus said – then the Spirit will ensure that we will remember them in times of difficulty and stress.

Father, a new world seems to be opening up to me. Thank You for showing me the importance of the words of Jesus. Help me in my meditations to think His thoughts after Him. In Jesus' name I pray. Amen.

What does 'the way' look like?

Carl Beech, UK Director of The Message Trust, speaker, author and church planter, introduces his new book, The Way.

I came to Christ from a completely unchurched background, and so I had no idea what it meant to follow Jesus. Over the years, by observing and listening to my pastors and leaders and by reading the Bible, I started to get really drawn to what it means to live according to Matthew 5 – to be full of grace, to be merciful, a peacemaker and so on. You see, we can have brilliant biblical knowledge, but sometimes lack in matters of the heart, character and spiritual disciplines. I wanted to cut to the core of what it means to follow Jesus, and the Beatitudes certainly do that.

This book is full of real-life stories of people like you and me who are living according to the Beatitudes today in one way or another. Their stories are real, raw and honest. The Beatitudes are so upside down, so counter-cultural that you can't expect an always easy life. But in return you open yourself up to be used by God, and have the promise of His blessing. I hope this book helps to challenge people, and get them excited all over again to live their lives completely for Jesus.

The Way is available from May 2017. To purchase, use the order form at the back of these notes or visit **www.cwr.org.uk/store**
ISBN: 978-1-78259-733-9

The word brought to life

FOR READING & MEDITATION – MATTHEW 25:31–46

*'For I was hungry and you gave me nothing to eat, I was thirsty
and you gave me nothing to drink' (v42)*

We spend one last day reflecting on the importance of knowing the Scriptures, particularly the things Jesus said, so that whenever we need instruction, guidance or encouragement the Holy Spirit can bring Jesus' words to mind.

A friend of mine regards his greatest achievement as memorising every word of Jesus in Scripture. I once asked him what it had meant to him in practical terms. He replied: 'Whenever I am faced with a difficulty in my life I find that the Holy Spirit brings to my remembrance some word of Jesus that relates to that situation and applies its healing balm to my heart.' As I have said before, the thing that acts as an anchor in my life and holds me steady in any storm that comes my way is the fact that I have spent a lifetime poring over the Scriptures. The Spirit uses my familiarisation of Scripture and applies the right passages to my heart and mind.

FURTHER STUDY

Matt. 7:24–29;
John 4:39–42;
Col. 1:3–8;
1 Pet. 1:22–23

1. What effect did Jesus' words have on the Samaritans?

2. How can Jesus' words come alive in us?

Permit a personal testimony at this point. I was brought up in a church in which there was strong resistance to what was then called 'the social gospel'. As Christians, I was told, we should focus people's attention on heaven and not be sidetracked by social issues. For years I veered away from becoming involved in anything to do with the social and regarded the spiritual and the social as being in conflict. One day, however, the Spirit pressed the words of today's text on my heart. In an instant I saw that there is no conflict between the spiritual and the social. In this case the spiritual is the social. The distinction is an invidious one. The Word was in my heart and the Spirit brought it to life.

God, help me meditate on Your Word so that it comes alive in me. Thank You, Holy Spirit, for Your wonderful ministry as my teacher and remembrancer. Amen.

A taste of what's ahead

FOR READING & MEDITATION – 2 CORINTHIANS 1:12–24

*'He... put his Spirit in our hearts as a deposit,
guaranteeing what is to come.' (v22)*

The ninth ministry of the Holy Spirit is to give us, as today's text tells us, a deposit or first instalment, guaranteeing what will be paid in full later. The Spirit deposits in our souls a taste of the banquet that lies ahead. Whenever we need encouragement, the Spirit is there to give us a glimpse of what's coming, enabling us to persevere in difficult times. We glimpse what's coming and persevere regardless of what is happening now. In the terrible days when slaves worked in the American plantations they sang a lot about heaven as they laboured under the lash of their masters. They could not enjoy their present experience but they could look forward with hope to what they were going to experience.

How wonderful it is to think that we have within our hearts a member of the Trinity whose task it is (among others) to give us a taste of what lies ahead. There's so much more to knowing God than we imagine. How important it is that we put aside our cynicism and wait consciously and deliberately for the Spirit to satisfy our souls with the enjoyment of God.

Anticipating heaven is not something that people talk much about. I wonder why! Is it because life is so good down here on earth – for those of us who live in relative prosperity anyway? Jonathan Edwards, the great revivalist, wrote, 'This life ought to be spent by us only as a journey to heaven.' Can you see what he is saying? We ought never to lose sight of our destination, for when we do then we tend to look at life from a temporal perspective rather than an eternal one. And to live with only a temporal perspective is to live dangerously.

FURTHER STUDY

Rom. 15:7–13;
2 Cor. 4:13–18

1. What effect does the Holy Spirit's power produce?

2. On what should we fix our eyes?

God, save me from seeing life merely from a temporal point of view. Please keep the vision of heaven ever before me. That, I know, is what Your Spirit seeks to help me do. May I co-operate, I pray. In Jesus' name. Amen.

The gentle voice within

FOR READING & MEDITATION – HEBREWS 12:1–13

'Let us fix our eyes on Jesus... who for the joy set before him endured the cross, scorning its shame' (v2)

Jesus once told His disciples, 'I am going... to prepare a place for you. And if I go and prepare a place for you, I will come back and take you to be with me' (John 14:2–3). And there is a voice in our soul, if we are ready to listen to it, that continually seeks to remind us of that glorious fact – the gentle voice of the Spirit.

In today's text the writer to the Hebrews tells us Jesus was kept moving forward in His earthly life by 'the joy set before him'. I feel sure that the Spirit who was in Him helped Him focus on that joy. Eugene Peterson's paraphrase of this section of Hebrews helps bring the meaning home to us: 'Keep your eyes on Jesus, who both began and finished this race we're in. Study how he did it. Because he never lost sight of where he was headed – that exhilarating finish in and with God – he could put up with anything along the way: cross, shame, whatever. And now he's there, in the place of honor, right alongside God. When you find yourselves flagging in your faith, go over that story again... That will shoot adrenaline into your souls!' (Heb. 12:2–3, *The Message*).

FURTHER STUDY

John 17:13–19;
2 Thess.
2:13–3:5

1. What does Jesus pray for His disciples?

2. What does Paul pray for the Thessalonians?

Are we seeing here the great secret of our Jesus' perseverance? I think so. He most certainly did not ignore the needs of His day, but He kept His gaze focused on what lay before Him – the joy of 'bringing many sons to glory' (Heb. 2:10). 'There is a voice in the heart of every true Christian,' says one writer, 'that calls us to the place that is reserved for us.' And he adds, 'The trouble is that we seldom hear that voice because we are too busy focusing on the things that are going on all around us.' As the poet put it, '[turn] round your faces, the best is yet to be.'

Father, I am so thankful that though I am part of this world, and have responsibilities here, my final destination is heaven. Help me not to neglect one for the other. In Jesus' name. Amen.

Next Issue

Confusion to Confidence

How can we believe that God is in control when world events appear to deny this? Why does He seemingly allow evil to reign and cause such suffering and damage?

These are the issues that Habakkuk had to grapple with centuries ago. And they are still relevant today where there is uncertainty, unrest and fear. By exploring the life of Habakkuk and the discoveries he made, we can learn, as he did, how to rise above confusion and face the world with confidence. Learning to trust in God's plan for the future, we can stand firm in difficult times and live each day with confidence in Him.

Every Day
with Jesus
JUL/AUG 2017

Confusion
to
Confidence

'Let us then approach
God's throne of grace
with confidence'
Hebrews 4:16

Be revived and refreshed by God's Word   CWR

Also available
as eBook/
eSubscription

Obtain your copy from CWR, a Christian bookshop or National Distributor.
If you would like to take out a subscription, see the order form at the back of these notes.

Are you listening?

FOR READING & MEDITATION – JOHN 13:1–17

'Jesus knew that the time had come for him to leave this world and go to the Father.' (v1)

We saw yesterday how Jesus sustained Himself in the midst of great opposition. He never lost sight of where He was heading. The passage before us today illuminates the point still further. John tells us that 'Jesus knew… he had come from God and was returning to God' (v3). The consciousness of where He had come from and where He was going enabled Him to deal with the present in a way that glorified God and illustrated for the disciples a lesson in humility.

I am convinced that one of the reasons why so many people give up rather than persevere in times of trial is because they have lost the anticipation of heaven. When I ask some Christians if they have ever heard the Spirit whispering this message in their hearts, 'Keep going, it won't be all that long now before you are home', they look at me as if I am talking in a foreign language. Why is this? It is because our lives are so crowded with activity that we have no time to listen to what the Spirit is saying to us.

It's interesting to me that Jesus ends every one of the seven messages to the churches in Revelation chapters 2–3 with words which could be paraphrased like this: 'Are you listening?' The issue isn't that God is not speaking; rather, the problem most often is that we're not listening. Throughout my life I have learned from mature Christians – Christians who took time to listen to the Spirit's voice and were ahead of me in the Christian race. I have discovered that in almost every one there was a great sense of responsibility for the work they had to do on earth, but there was also a clear focus on the destiny that was ahead.

FURTHER STUDY

Phil. 1:19–26;
1 Tim. 6:11–19

1. How did Paul view his own death?

2. What counsel does Paul give Timothy concerning the future?

Gracious Father, forgive me if my soul is so filled with other sounds that I cannot hear the sound of Your Spirit speaking in my heart. Forgive me and may Your Spirit guide my life. In Jesus' name. Amen.

Groaning within

FOR READING & MEDITATION – ROMANS 8:18–27

*'we... who have the firstfruits of the Spirit, groan inwardly as we wait
eagerly for our adoption as sons' (v23)*

Today we return to a passage we considered earlier to pick up on the point the apostle is making, namely that all who have responded to the call of Jesus have found new freedom and that their spirits are alive to God. This means that we can be free from all fear and have our minds set on what the Spirit desires (Rom. 8:5). The Christian life is a life of release, freedom and joy. Indeed, as we saw earlier, joy is the second aspect of the fruit of the Spirit.

How intriguing, then, to read that despite this freedom we groan inwardly – we groan for our adoption as sons and the redemption of our bodies. In other words, although as Christians we enjoy our salvation, there is within us a Spirit-created groan that reminds us that, as the old song says, 'This world is not our home, we're just a-passing through.' This tension between joy and an inward groan is one with which a Christian lives daily – joy at receiving the gift of eternal life and a groan because of our knowledge that we live in a world adrift from God.

FURTHER STUDY

1 Cor. 15:49–58;
Phil. 3:17–21;
Heb. 9:23–28

1. Who are we waiting for?

2. What are we waiting for?

If the Spirit is allowed to work in our hearts as He desires, then He will quicken us to 'wait eagerly for our adoption as sons'. Did you notice the word eagerly? Is there an eagerness in you (that is not escapism) for the day when everything will be set right? Here there is something wrong with everything; there (in heaven) there will be nothing wrong with anything.

Consider this: if the Spirit is in our hearts to give us a taste of what is to come, why is it that the things of time loom so large in our lives and the things of eternity draw no more energy from us than a yawn? Something doesn't add up.

Lord, forgive me if I am more interested in temporal things than the things of eternity. Help me, I pray, to have a greater eagerness for heaven. In Jesus' name. Amen.

Has someone let you down?

FOR READING & MEDITATION – 2 CORINTHIANS 5:1–10

'if the earthly tent we live in is destroyed, we have a building from God, an eternal house in heaven' (v1)

For one more day we reflect on the truth that one reason amongst others why the Spirit is in our hearts is to whet our appetites for the day when we shall be gathered together with Christ in heaven. Brent Curtis and John Eldridge, in their book *The Sacred Romance*, claim that the anticipation of heaven – a Spirit-created desire – enables us more than anything else does to deal with the pain we experience as a result of living in a fallen world.

Has someone let you down recently? How do you handle your life when this happens? You can retreat into cynicism, become angry, break the relationship with the person concerned and console yourself that they will never be able to do that to you again. A better way, say Brent Curtis and John Eldridge, is to allow that pain to remind you that in heaven there will be no problems – no pain, no death, no suffering, no difficult relationships. Some would say this is opting out or denial. But it isn't. You would, of course, be opting out or in denial if you pretended you were not hurt, for integrity requires that whatever we feel must be faced. So, after facing the hurt and feeling it, let it lead you to the fact that up ahead all will be made right. The anticipation of what lies ahead relieves the suffering we experience down here.

FURTHER STUDY

Titus 2:11–15;
1 Pet. 1:3–9

1. How can we stir up the holy longing for home?

2. What perspective does Peter give to present suffering?

Our heart can be restored to life and the smallest thing a reminder of heaven if we ask one simple question: What is this telling me about where I really belong? St Augustine said: 'The whole life of the good Christian is a holy longing.' The more eagerly we long for home, the less difficult are the sufferings we go through at this present time.

Dear God, I see the truth. Please help me to take it to heart. Without avoiding my responsibilities here on earth, may I have a holy longing for home. In Jesus' name. Amen.

No need for teachers?

FOR READING & MEDITATION – 1 JOHN 2:18–27

'the anointing you received from him remains in you, and you do not need anyone to teach you.' (v27)

The tenth ministry of the Spirit, as today's reading illustrates, is to anoint us so that we are enabled to distinguish between deception and error. We have touched on the aspect of the Holy Spirit as our teacher and remembrancer before, but we look at it now from another perspective.

At the time of John's writing, there were a group of people called Gnostics (or 'knowing ones') who maintained that the teaching of the apostles was to be supplemented by a 'higher knowledge' which they, the Gnostics, claimed to possess. This 'higher knowledge' was gained (so they believed) by a superior intuition which set them apart from others. John tells his readers that what the Spirit had taught them through the words of Jesus and the teaching of the apostles was not just adequate for salvation but was the only reliable truth.

FURTHER STUDY

2 Tim. 1:13–18; Jude 17–25

1. What safeguards us as believers?

2. How are we kept from falling?

The statement, 'You do not need anyone to teach you,' does not mean that teachers are not needed in the Church and that we can simply depend on the Spirit for illumination. As we have seen, Scripture clearly speaks of the ministry of pastors and teachers in the Church, so John is not contradicting this. What he is saying is that we do not need teachers who add to the revelation already given by Jesus and His apostles. All that we need to know to live a Christ-like life is found in the Scriptures.

The Holy Spirit anoints believers so that they develop a capacity to perceive divine truth – truth which has already been revealed. You can be sure that if I were to attempt to teach you anything contrary to Scripture the Holy Spirit would ring a bell in your heart and warn: 'Beware, you are being led astray... this is not in accordance with the truth.'

Holy Spirit, how glad I am for this divine anointing that comes from You and safeguards us against error. I love the truth and want always to live in accordance with it. In Jesus' name. Amen.

'The ring of truth'

FOR READING & MEDITATION – 1 JOHN 3:1–10

'Dear children, do not let anyone lead you astray.' (v7)

John's command not to let anyone lead us astray is linked to that which he refers to in 1 John chapter 2 that we mentioned yesterday, namely that we have an anointing from the Holy Spirit which enables 'us to perceive divine truth: 'the anointing you received from him remains in you, and you do not need anyone to teach you' (1 John 2:27). If we keep close to Scripture and allow the Holy Spirit to have His way in our hearts, then we will not go astray and be misled by false doctrines.

The Holy Spirit's anointing teaches us 'about all things' (1 John 2:27). Does this mean the anointing of the Spirit makes us 'know-alls'? I believe not! Instead, it means that everything has been made known that we need to know in order to live a life that pleases God. Take, for example, this statement: 'The Gnostics believed that eternal salvation was to be gained by climbing the ladder of thirty-six steps to God by inward knowledge.' What do you think about that? I strongly suspect that the Spirit will caution you that there is nothing in Scripture about climbing thirty-six steps to get to God. Jesus is the way and the only way (see John 14:6).

The Gnostics also believed that people could use their bodies for illicit sexual pleasure because the physical had no connection to the spiritual. What will the Spirit who abides in your heart tell you about that? He will remind you that your body is the temple of the Holy Spirit (1 Cor. 6:19).

J.B. Phillips called this 'the ring of truth'. How grateful we are for this great ministry of the Holy Spirit who keeps us walking in the truth and light.

FURTHER STUDY

Psa. 86:11–12;
Prov. 12:13–22;
1 Thess. 4:1–8;
Rev. 2:12–17

1. How are we kept on the paths of purity?

2. What warning and what promise is given to the Pergamum church?

Holy Spirit, I am most grateful that You have come to me, and not only come to me but that You indwell me. What joy it is to know that You keep me walking in the truth. Amen.

He is the Truth

FOR READING & MEDITATION – ROMANS 6:15–23

'But thanks be to God that... you wholeheartedly obeyed the form of teaching to which you were entrusted.' (v17)

Over the past few days we have looked at an error that existed in the Early Church – the error of Gnosticism. There are some forms of Gnosticism still abroad in the Church today, particularly dualism – the separation of the spiritual and the material.

A church leader was once brought before the elders of the church because of his adultery. He excused his behaviour by saying it wasn't he himself that had done it, but the old Adam, his carnal nature, that had committed the sinful act. The elders saw through this and told him he would not be able to partake in any ministry until he had repented of his sin. The case of David's adultery with Bathsheba in 2 Samuel 11 and 12 shows, tragically, it is possible to suppress the voice of the Spirit and live in denial, as David did for a number of months. Thankfully, through Nathan's barbed parable, he got through David's defences and he was brought to repentance.

Earlier we saw that the Holy Spirit not only teaches truth but is Himself the Spirit of truth (John 14:16–17). What we receive from Him is not truth alone – the bare facts – but, since He is the Spirit of truth, we receive the facts plus the power to live according to those facts. We might say that the Holy Spirit establishes a private 'School of the Spirit' within us when we are converted, in which He sets about teaching us all things and guiding us into all truth (John 16:13). A human teacher can teach us the truth yet not guide us into it, because he or she may know the truth only in theory. The Spirit guides us into the truth because He is the Truth. And He is not content until the truth not only reaches into our spirit but takes possession of us.

FURTHER STUDY

Micah 3:5–12;
Luke 2:25–32;
Acts 13:4–12

1. How was Simeon led by the Spirit?

2. How was Paul enabled to expose deception?

Father, I see that I am a trainee of the Spirit. May I be an eager, responsive student in the 'School of the Spirit', for if I do not learn how to live according to the truth, then I do not live – period. Amen.

Three steps to transformation

FOR READING & MEDITATION – 1 THESSALONIANS 1:1–10

'our gospel came... not simply with words, but also with power, with the Holy Spirit and with deep conviction.' (v5)

Something more is needed than mere human knowledge or education to deal with the struggles of the soul. We need to learn to live in the 'School of the Spirit' in which the teacher is the Holy Spirit Himself.

Many contemporary therapies, for example, undertake to cure the soul's problems through knowledge. The psychologist Carl Jung said that to cure the ills of the soul four things are necessary: confession, explanation, education, and transformation. The two middle steps – explanation and education – alone aren't able to sustain the last – transformation. They can provide alleviation, reformation, even realignment, but only occasionally lasting transformation. Psychiatry is very good at symptom relief but rarely brings about fundamental change in the depths of the personality.

In the private 'School of the Spirit', matters are much different, however. Four steps are also taught: confession, surrender, acceptance, and transformation. Only these first three steps are capable of producing the fourth. Confession involves bringing everything out into the open and requires complete honesty with yourself and with God. Surrender is the transfer of the central allegiance from the self to God. Acceptance is dependence and trust on the Spirit, who enables us to rise to live the life to which Jesus calls His followers. These three steps lead to transformation, since God's Spirit is then free to operate. There is nothing the Holy Spirit delights in doing more than transforming the honest, surrendered and receptive soul.

FURTHER STUDY

Psa. 143:1–12;
Rom. 8:28–30;
2 Cor. 3:7–18

1. How does the psalmist show himself receptive to God?

2. How does Paul describe Christian transformation?

Holy Spirit, gracious teacher and transformer, I have taken the steps of confession, surrender and acceptance. No longer will I try to transform myself. Instead I will look to You to do it. In Jesus' name. Amen.

Divine illumination

FOR READING & MEDITATION – PSALM 119:17–24

'Open my eyes that I may see wonderful things in your law.' (v18)

For one more day we reflect on the thought that every Christian is anointed by the Spirit to perceive God's truth as it has been revealed in Jesus. The enlightening ministry of the Spirit which we have been talking about is often referred to as 'divine illumination'. Notice that the Spirit gives 'illumination', not 'revelation'. Sometimes you will hear a church leader say that they have received a new 'revelation' in connection with some passage of Scripture, but what they mean is that they have had fresh 'illumination'. There is no 'new' truth to be added to Scripture (hence no further revelation).

However, illumination is needed to understand truth that we may not have fully grasped. Almost every day as I read my Bible I discover things that have been there all the time but which have previously not been illuminated. And I am so glad the Spirit illuminates them gradually, for if I learned all there is to know at once my soul would be overwhelmed. He ensures that this illumination keeps pace with my readiness to know more of God and His Word. What an expert illuminator the Holy Spirit is. And, amazingly, in this 'School of the Spirit' there is round-the-clock tutelage. The Spirit abides in us, which means He is available to us twenty-four hours a day!

In this private 'School of the Spirit' something different takes place: the teacher and the pupil become one – one in knowledge, one in love, one in action. The degree to which this happens depends, of course, on the willingness of the pupil to respond and receive. All that is required to enter this school is co-operation. You supply the willingness; He supplies the power.

FURTHER STUDY

Psa. 119: 121–136; 2 Cor. 8:1–7

1. How willing was the psalmist to perceive God's truth?

2. How did the Macedonians exceed their own ability?

Father, I realise that in the 'School of the Spirit' I, a very ordinary person, am joined to someone who is extraordinary, and so I experience results out of all proportion to my innate abilities. I am so grateful. Amen.

Poured-out love

FOR READING & MEDITATION – ROMANS 5:1–11

'And hope does not disappoint us, because God has poured out his love into our hearts by the Holy Spirit' (v5)

The final ministry of the Spirit which we shall consider is His task of pouring God's love into our hearts. Sadly, many people find it hard to believe they are loved unconditionally. During the many years I have been involved in counselling I have met hundreds of people who have told me their stories and confided that they have never received from their parents, friends or family the love they longed to know.

The truth is, of course, that no one on earth has ever loved us in the way our hearts long for. Parents are not enough, friends are not enough, a husband or wife is not enough. There is something deep within every single one of us that longs for a love greater than anything another human being can give. As in everything that matters to the proper functioning of our souls, we are dependent on the Holy Spirit. He alone assures us that we are fully loved and that no matter who may not love us, we are loved by the One whose love surpasses human love. And the Spirit convinces us of this truth by pouring the Father's love into our hearts.

It is my belief that our inability to deal with the problems that come our way is due in no small measure to feeling unloved. When I feel loved, something powerful and profound happens at the core of my being. I feel I can face any problem that comes my way, rise above grudges, shrug off any attack, concentrate on my work. But when I do not feel loved then everything seems harder and more problematic. So important is love to our functioning as human beings that unless the Spirit pours it into our hearts, then though we are living, we are not living abundantly.

FURTHER STUDY

Rom. 8:31–39;
1 Thess. 4:9–10;
1 John 2:28–3:3

1. In what should the Thessalonians excel?

2. What is lavished upon the children of God?

God my Father, You who fashioned us in the depths of our being for love, and who through the Holy Spirit radiates that love, fill me to overflowing with that love today. In Jesus' name. Amen.

What drives you?

FOR READING & MEDITATION – 2 CORINTHIANS 5:11–21

'For Christ's love compels us, because we are convinced that one died for all, and therefore all died.' (v14)

Why is love so important to effective human life and living? The simple answer is because we were designed by our Creator to first respond to the love which comes from Him, and then to give out love to others. The whole purpose of our existence on earth is to have loving involvement with God and loving involvement with others.

The 'power pack' that God has placed at the core of our personalities and which provides us with the energy and motivation to move into life is designed to operate under and be energised by divine love. Since the fall of Adam and Eve in the Garden of Eden, sin has damaged the original human design, and now, when we come into the world, we are motivated not by divine love but by self-love. Salvation reconnects us, through the cross, to the love for which we were made. If that love does not fill our souls, then we are like finely-tuned automobiles running on low grade petrol and unable to perform according to the designer's original specifications.

In the passage before us today, the apostle Paul tells us that we are compelled by the love of Christ. The Greek word Paul uses here is *sunecho*, which can be translated 'mastered', 'controlled', or even 'monopolised'. Please allow me at this stage to ask you a personal question: What motivates you in your Christian life? What makes you tick, so to speak? If tests could be done today to find out what energises you, would it be that you are 'fully persuaded' by the truth that you are divinely loved? The love of Christ poured into his heart by the Holy Spirit was certainly what gave Paul his great spiritual energy. Nothing else, in spiritual terms I mean, is as life changing. Nothing.

FURTHER STUDY

Psa. 116:1–9;
Luke 7:40–50;
John 5:41–47

1. Why did the psalmist love God?

2. For what did Jesus commend the sinful woman?

Loving and merciful God, I know that a degree of self-love must lie at my heart, but let the love for You be stronger than anything else. In Jesus' name. Amen.

Hiding from love

FOR READING & MEDITATION – 1 JOHN 4:16–21

*'There is no fear in love. But perfect love drives out fear,
because fear has to do with punishment.' (v18)*

Despite the readiness of the Holy Spirit to pour the Father's love into our hearts, there are countless Christians who find it difficult to receive that love. In fact, they find it difficult to receive any kind of love, whether it is human or divine. Often this is due in part to difficulties they encountered in their developmental years.

Sometimes the difficulty is that the love shown to them while they were growing up was a conditional love – the kind of love typified with a qualification such as: 'I will love you if you do this... if you pass the examination... if you don't give me any trouble.' With others the problem is that they did not receive love consistently. One day they would be shown love and the next day indifference – and for no apparent reason. They learned it was not safe to receive love and so they closed their hearts to all approaching love. They now hide from love out of fear that it might not prove genuine. Then there are others who were brought up in an atmosphere where love was expressed only in words and there was little or no non-verbal communication, such as hugs and caresses.

Those who find it difficult to receive love often try to put themselves in the position where they are the givers and not the receivers. One writer who says he finds it difficult to receive love puts it like this: 'I find it's safer to give, never to be in the one-down, vulnerable position of truly needing anything. It's difficult to meaningfully ask the Holy Spirit to penetrate the exact centre of my heart, find the empty hole and fill it with God's love. It seems so needy and weak.' It's sad that someone should be afraid of love.

FURTHER STUDY

John 21:15–17;
2 Cor. 6:11–13;
Eph. 3:14–21;
1 Thess. 2:6–9

1. How was Peter to show his love for Christ?

2. How can we grasp the love of Christ?

Father, if there are any blocks within me that hinder me from receiving love, whether it is Your love or the love of others, then remove them I pray. Free me from fear and I will be really free. Amen.

The great divide

FOR READING & MEDITATION – 1 JOHN 4:7–16

'And so we know and rely on the love God has for us.' (v16)

Without the work of the Spirit, who pours the love of the Father into our hearts, we cannot feel fully loved at the core of our hearts, and we will fail to live in the way we were designed. What then happens in the hearts of Christians who are unable to receive love is that they work hard to manage their lives, doing all the right things, and trying to get along on whatever kind of love is shown to them.

Not long ago, I talked to a Christian who was in this situation and he said: 'From the pulpit of my church I continually hear about the fact that God loves me but it excites me no more than the sunshine or the air. There is no wonder in it. "The love of God" to me is just a phrase and nothing more. Yet I know He loves me and has died for my sins. I know it but I do not feel it.' At once I realised I was talking to a person who had some emotional obstacle that prevented him from accepting love. He then told me the story of his childhood, which almost moved me to tears.

As we continued talking I told him how Teresa of Avila, who at one time was a very practical person and more comfortable giving love than receiving it, came to a new place in her spiritual life. In the Carmelite convent where she was a nun she noticed a picture of Jesus being scourged. She had seen it hundreds of times before, but suddenly she saw it as she had never seen it before. She saw God suffering – suffering out of love for her. It sent her to her knees and she wept hot adoring tears of love. That was the great divide of her life. The way in which people come to be receptive to God's love varies, but very often it happens at Calvary.

FURTHER STUDY

Luke 23:38–49;
Gal. 6:14–16

1. What could be seen and heard at the foot of the cross?

2. In what did Paul boast?

Father, bring me once again to Calvary I pray. Enrapture my soul with a new revelation of Your love. Help me linger again at the foot of the cross, for there Your love finds its most burning expression. In Jesus' name. Amen.

'Not enough containers'

FOR READING & MEDITATION – TITUS 3:1–11

*'But when the kindness and love of God our Saviour appeared,
he saved us' (vv4–5)*

O n our last day together, our final thought is this: the Spirit works in the lives of those who find themselves prevented from receiving love by doing what He did for Teresa of Avila – He gives them a supernatural revelation of the cross.

If I am speaking to someone who finds it hard to be loved, then this is God's message to you: attend to the cross. Sit before it. Meditate on it. Open your heart and mind to what Jesus did for you there. Remember that the love of God finds its most burning expression at Calvary. Forget about everything else for a little while and think about Christ's great suffering for you. Give yourself to this for as long as you can. God alone knows the love of God, and only God the Holy Spirit can reveal it. You do the possible by waiting before Him and He will do what is impossible for you by taking the scales from your eyes. The more you receive His love, the more your own love will flame in response. Your love for Him is a response to His love for you. That's what John meant when he said, 'We love because he first loved us' (1 John 4:19). We cannot command the vision of God's love which in turn removes the obstacles that prevent us receiving it, but we can put ourselves in the way of it. Wait at Calvary. Linger there.

FURTHER STUDY

Mark 15:33–41;
Rev. 1:4–8

1. Of what was the centurion sure?

2. Give thanks along with John to Him who loves us.

What I am talking about might sound mystical, but this type of contemplation brings great spiritual rewards. I pray that whether or not you have found it difficult to receive love, you might be given such a great awareness of the divine love that, in Eugene Peterson's words, 'we can't round up enough containers to hold everything God generously pours into our lives through the Holy Spirit' (Rom. 5:5, *The Message*).

Father, help me to live beneath the shadow of the cross, for it is there that I see the extent of Your love. Nothing in me gave rise to it, and nothing in me can extinguish it. Your love is from everlasting to everlasting. I am so thankful. Amen.

Order form

4 Easy Ways To Order

1. Phone in your credit card order: **01252 784700** (Mon–Fri, 9.30am – 5pm)
2. Visit our online store at **www.cwr.org.uk/store**
3. Send this form together with your payment to: **CWR, Waverley Abbey House, Waverley Lane, Farnham, Surrey GU9 8EP**
4. Visit a Christian bookshop

For a list of our National Distributors, who supply countries outside the UK, visit **www.cwr.org.uk/distributors**

Your Details (required for orders and donations)

Full Name:	CWR ID No. (if known):
Home Address:	
	Postcode:
Telephone No. (for queries):	Email:

Publications

TITLE	QTY	PRICE	TOTAL
		Total Publications	

UK P&P: up to £24.99 = **£2.99**; £25.00 and over = **FREE**

Elsewhere P&P: up to £10 = **£4.95**; £10.01 – £50 = **£6.95**; £50.01 – £99.99 = **£10**; £100 and over = **£30**

Total Publications and P&P (please allow 14 days for delivery) **A**

All CWR adult Bible reading notes are also available in **eBook** and **email subscription** format. Visit **www.cwr.org.uk** for further information.

Subscriptions* (non direct debit)

	QTY	PRICE (including P&P)			TOTAL
		UK	Europe	Elsewhere	
Every Day with Jesus (1yr, 6 issues)		£15.95	£19.95		
Large Print Every Day with Jesus (1yr, 6 issues)		£15.95	£19.95	Please contact	
Inspiring Women Every Day (1yr, 6 issues)		£15.95	£19.95	nearest	
Life Every Day (Jeff Lucas) (1yr, 6 issues)		£15.95	£19.95	National	
Mettle: 15–18s (1yr, 3 issues)		£14.50	£16.60	Distributor	
YP's: 11–14s (1yr, 6 issues)		£15.95	£19.95	or CWR direct	
Topz: 7–11s (1yr, 6 issues)		£15.95	£19.95		
Cover to Cover Every Day		Email subscription only, to order visit online store.			

Total Subscriptions (subscription prices already include postage and packing) **B**

Please circle which issue you would like your subscription to commence from:

JAN/FEB MAR/APR MAY/JUN JUL/AUG SEP/OCT NOV/DEC Mettle JAN–APR MAY–AUG SEP–DEC

Only use this section for subscriptions paid for by credit/debit card or cheque. For Direct Debit subscriptions see overleaf.

We promise to never share your details with other charities. By giving us your personal information, you agree that we may use this to send you information about the ministry of CWR. If you do not want to receive further information by post, please tick here. ☐

Continued overleaf >>

<< See previous page for start of order form

Payment Details

☐ I enclose a cheque/PO made payable to CWR for the amount of: **£** _____

☐ Please charge my credit/debit card.

Cardholder's Name (in BLOCK CAPITALS) _____

Card No. ☐☐☐☐ ☐☐☐☐ ☐☐☐☐ ☐☐☐☐

Expires End ☐☐ ☐☐   Security Code ☐☐☐

Gift to CWR   ☐ Please send me an acknowledgement of my gift   **C** [   ]

Gift Aid (your home address required, see overleaf)

giftaid it   I am a UK taxpayer and want CWR to reclaim the tax on all my donations for the four years prior to this y **and on** all donations I make from the date of this Gift Aid declaration until further notice.*

Taxpayer's Full Name (in BLOCK CAPITALS) _____

Signature _____   **Date** _____

* I am a UK taxpayer and understand that if I pay less Income Tax and/or Capital Gains Tax than the amount of Gift Aid claimed on all my donations in tha year it is my responsibility to pay any difference.

GRAND TOTAL (Total of A, B & C)   [   ]

Subscriptions by Direct Debit (UK bank account holders only)

One-year subscriptions cost £15.95 (except *Mettle*: £14.50) and include UK delivery. Please tick relevant boxes and fill in the form below

☐ *Every Day with Jesus* (1yr, 6 issues)
☐ Large Print *Every Day with Jesus* (1yr, 6 issues)
☐ *Inspiring Women Every Day* (1yr, 6 issues)
☐ *Life Every Day* (Jeff Lucas) (1yr, 6 issues)

☐ *Mettle*: 15–18s (1yr, 3 issues)
☐ *YP's*: 11–14s (1yr, 6 issues)
☐ *Topz*: 7–11s (1yr, 6 issues)

Issue to commence from
☐ Jan/Feb ☐ Jul/Aug   *Mettle* ☐ Jan–Apr
☐ Mar/Apr ☐ Sep/Oct   ☐ May–Aug
☐ May/Jun ☐ Nov/Dec   ☐ Sep–Dec

CWR Instruction to your Bank or Building Society to pay by Direct Debit   DIRE Deb

Please fill in the form and send to: CWR, Waverley Abbey House, Waverley Lane, Farnham, Surrey GU9 8EP

Name and full postal address of your Bank or Building Society

To: The Manager _____ Bank/Building Society

Address _____

_____

_____ Postcode _____

Name(s) of Account Holder(s)

_____

Branch Sort Code

☐☐ ☐☐ ☐☐

Bank/Building Society Account Number

☐☐☐☐☐☐☐☐

Originator's Identification Number

| 4 | 2 | 0 | 4 | 8 | 7 |

Reference

| | | | | | | | | | |

Instruction to your Bank or Building Society

Please pay CWR Direct Debits from the account detailed in this In subject to the safeguards assured by the Direct Debit Guarantee. I understand that this Instruction may remain with CWR and, if so will be passed electronically to my Bank/Building Society.

Signature(s)

_____

_____

Date _____

Banks and Building Societies may not accept Direct Debit Instructions for some types of account